# FABIO'S ADVENTURES AS A CHILD

FABIO DUSETTI

DIAMOND MEDIA PRESS CO.
1-888-322-7392
https://www.diamondmediapressco.com/



By Fabio Dusetti



ISBN Paperback: 978-1-951302-36-8

# Contents

## INTRODUCTION

I WANT TO DISCUSS A SITUATION of an offspring who is not old enough to leave home and others and what it is like to be taken away from home at the age of seven to earn one's living.

In northern Italy, soon after World War II ended, food was so scarce that the ration coupons were of no use. The local shops simply didn't have the elementary goods in stock that people had ration coupons to buy. The farmers were the only people who still had some food. In sheer desperation, a mother took her seven-year-old son, Fabio, to a strange family in a village some distance from home, where he could earn his own living. She did the identical thing to all his brothers. They reunited once a year for the Christmas and New Year festivities.

This story is just different from anything else I have ever heard. When have you ever heard of a seven-year-old becoming a cowboy, and above all, a cowboy without a horse he could ride? This is the story of how Fabio guided and controlled his herd like a sheep dog manipulates his flock. How he pampered and groomed his herd nearly on a daily basis. How he was exploited to the point of being hindered from going to school on seventy-seven occasions during just one school year at a strange school where even a teacher had it in for him. Then, a smile from a girl in his class penetrated his heart and made him feel on top of the world.

In the summer, he ended up looking after animals on the Alpe di Siusi, which is the largest high-altitude Alpine meadow in Europe. When sleeping in the hay all summer, the indescribable scent of mountain flowers glided him into cloud nine. After Fabio left school, he couldn't find an apprenticeship position for the trade he dreamed of learning. So, at the age of fourteen, he abandoned his motherland to see what the rest of the world had to offer.

# CHAPTER ONE

IN 1942, I, FABIO, WAS BORN in Trento and lived in a northern Italian village called Laghetti. When World War II was in its last year. I wasn't even three years old at the time, but I remember being in a place where there were loads of grown-up people. They were all standing, and I could only see legs all around me. Later, as I got a bit older, I was told that it was an air-raid shelter. It was a U-shaped tunnel dug into the mountain to give the villagers some protection from the bombings by the Allies. This area of Italy was occupied by the German troops and was also the principal withdrawal valley for their final withdrawal. A large number of German troops withdrawing from the Italian liberators would have returned home using this valley. Leaflets were being dropped by the Allies during the day, informing the population not to leave lights on at night time. Lights at night time would attract bombings. In fact, we had lived in the same street where the air raid shelter was and just a few hundred meters further towards the village. After five bombs had been dropped on the village, as soon as the bombers were heard, people ran to the shelter. Thanks to the shelter, there weren't any human losses during the bombings.

My oldest brother, Mario, had been called to the Mussolini youth camps. My other brothers, second and third oldest, Lodovico and Pino, weren't at home, while the fourth oldest, Ignaz, was with us.

We lived in a rented house. I can faintly remember that there was water coming from under the entrance door to the apartment. Again, as I was a little bigger, I was informed that it was the landlord who did it because he wanted us to leave.

After this episode, I can remember living in a wooden building at the opposite end of the village. This wooden building was in a large excavation. From there, earth had been taken for the strengthening of the riverbanks. The big rocks had been left scattered around many times higher than the wooden building. I think that it was a building used as a barracks by the Germans who had occupied Italy.

The wooden barracks had the entrance from the main door to a corridor that went the length of the building. Then, from the corridor, doors opened into the different rooms.

At the right side of this barracks, there was a stable and an outside toilet. A goat was kept there for the daily milk needed for my family. There was also a sheep and chickens. I had four brothers, all older than me: Mario, Lodovico, Pino, and Ignaz. My brother Ignaz, who was nearest to my age, had to take the animals to graze in the woods above the excavation.

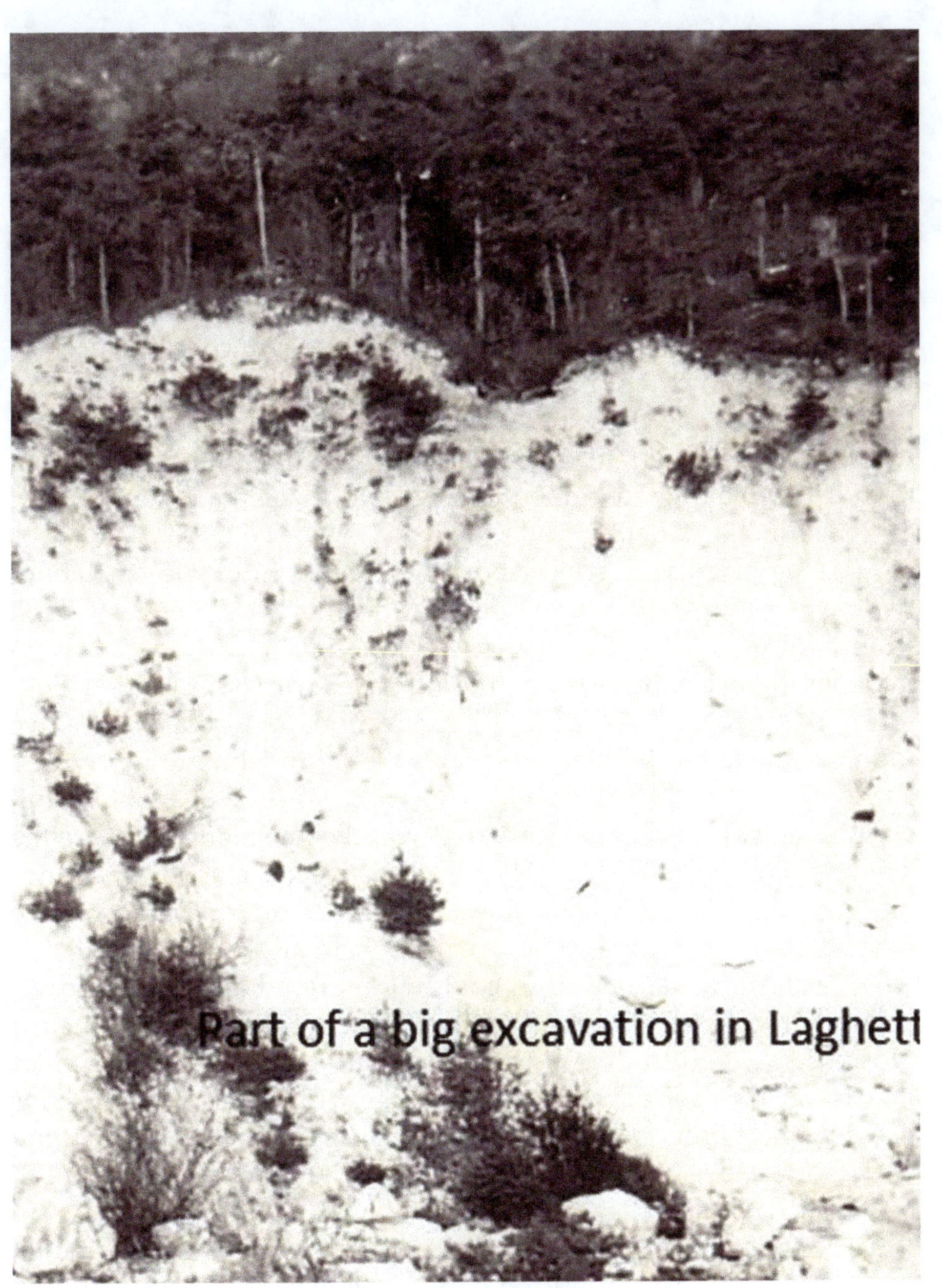


*(This is a small part of the excavation)*

I went with Ignaz as well, with bare feet, shorts, a shirt with short sleeves which was tucked into the trousers, and braces to hold the trousers up. I can't remember if I was asked to go along or if I went to have my brother's company.

To get to the woods, we had to go to the beginning of the excavation on one side or the other. At times, in the woods, we met other boys from the neighborhood with their goats. Occasionally, we started playing and forgot about the animals, and when we remembered them, they were nowhere to be seen. In consequence, we went looking for them in different directions. The first one to find them would guide them back to where we had been playing and would call the others to let them know that the animals had been found. The playing continued, but we had to keep a better lookout for the animals.

One of these neighbor boys was called Lino. He was about two years older than me, but for me, he was much bigger than I. I don't know if at that time the war was finished or not. I can remember that we children kept finding boxes with ammunition close to the rocks that were in the big excavation, and occasionally, we found a rifle as well. The bigger boys would try shooting the rifles, and each time, they would fall over backwards. The shooting fun wouldn't last long. Some grown-up would come along and take the rifle and ammunition away. The next time we found a box of ammunition, we would only take some cartridges and hide the rest. Then when a grown-up came along, we gave them all we had on us.

After a while, the rifles couldn't be found anymore, and we still had loads of cartridges. We liked to hear the bang from the explosion. As we didn't have any rifles, the bigger boys would place a cartridge on a rock and hit the cartridge with a hammer. The boys present stood around the rock while the cartridge got hit. Thinking back to those events makes me realize how lucky we all were not to be hit by the bullets that came out of the cartridge. The fact is, we always got left with a squashed, empty cartridge. Therefore, the bullet must have passed through the gaps in between the boys standing around the rock.

Once, to pass the time, we went to the railway line and placed cartridges close to one another on the metal rail for a long distance. Then, we would walk home and listen for a train to come. The trains didn't run regularly, and there were only cargo trains that we would observe. It was the railway line that went from the Brenner to Verona, and we would put the cartridges on the rails at the position thirty kilometers south of Bolzano. Then, when the train did come, it sounded just like a machine gun firing.

The train stopped, and we all went hiding even though we were a long way from the railway line. We thought that the driver would have told our parents. The driver, in fact, must have cleared the cartridges off the railway line. After a while, the train restarted and moved on without the shooting noise.

Then came a time that Lino kept teasing me about my mother having a big belly. To me, she was just my mother, and I didn't notice her having a big belly. I didn't know what he was talking about. Then, in 1946, my little brother, Klaus, appeared. I was then nearly four years old and didn't understand what that meant. Nothing changed until he got a bit bigger. My mother showed me how to spoon feed him. I think that spoon feeding my small brother was, in fact, my first official job.

My bigger brother, Pino, who is five years older than me, had to spoon feed my brother, Ignaz, and myself. The three eldest brothers weren't often to be seen. I didn't know why they weren't at home every day. My oldest brother, Mario, and second oldest, Lodovico, were, in fact, rarely to be seen.

There was a period when a friend of Mario, Walter, was staying with us. In the corridor where we lived, Mario and Walter had fitted a swing on the exposed ceiling joists. In the corridor and stable, there was no ceiling, and I could see the underside of the roof. On occasions, they sat me on the swing and pushed me. I got pushed so hard that I went extremely high up. In fact, it was so high that it took my breath away on the descent. Then one day, Mario's friend, Walter, was gone, and I have never seen him again.

The barracks we lived in had a roof covered in felt. When it rained, it leaked regularly in various places. From the woods above the excavation, repair patches could be seen scattered around the roof.

My only memory from kindergarten is having had to go to sleep in the afternoon. All the children had to fold their arms on their desks and lay their heads on their arms to go to sleep. I can't remember if I went alone to the kindergarten or if someone took me there. In a small village with no traffic or other dangers, I can imagine that I went home alone.

My family also had a piece of land that was about half an hour's walk from our home. The land had mainly vineyards, some peaches, and some spare ground for vegetables, corn, and potatoes, which were grown on rotation. If my mother worked in that field, she wouldn't have had the time to collect me from the kindergarten. It probably finished at the same time as the school. Therefore, my brother would have taken me home.

My father was and wasn't at home. He wasn't at home regularly like one would expect a father to be. He worked away from home, and at that time, he must have lived away and came home on occasions, just like my bigger brothers. It wasn't that easy to walk daily for hours to go to work and return in the evening.

As I got a bit bigger, it was me who had to take the animals grazing after I got home from school. I remember having been alone often at home despite having had so many brothers. It seemed that I was now the only one taking the animals grazing after school and during the summer holidays. At times, I also had to spoon feed my brother, Claudio.

One day, there were three brothers at home and my father. The third oldest brother, Pino, the fourth oldest, Ignaz, and me. Pino had seen his very first film in the cinema. All three of us were in a double bed, and Pino started to tell Ignaz and me about the story about the film he had seen. My father was sleeping in another room. After a while of Pino telling us the story, my father called out, "Be quiet. I can't sleep."

After a while, in a soft voice, Pino continued to tell us the exiting story. Then my father repeated his request. Ignaz and I were interested in hearing the end of the story and compelled Pino to continue. My father had enough and came with his trouser belt in his hand and whipped Pino's back with it. For days after that, when we went to bed, we could see the long belt imprint down Pino's back. That was the only time that I know of that my father hit one of us boys.

Occasionally, my father used to sit me on his lap or on one of his knees. Then he normally rubbed his unshaven chin on my face. It didn't hurt, but I didn't like it, and it made me go away from him. On Sundays, he used to sharpen his folding razor on a leather strap before shaving.

The habit was that we all would go to church on Sundays. My mother took one of us brothers to the first mass. The other brothers went with our father to the big mass. After the mass, one of us brothers went to the local shop to get whatever Mother had asked us to get. The cost of what we bought was registered in a book the shopkeeper held.

After mass, my father went to the local pub, which was next door to the alimentary shop. In consequence, he used to come home late for lunch and partially drunk. That used to make my mother furious. What made it even worse was the fact that he used to go to the local shop and get macaroni, the pasta with the big holes. It was inserted in open brown paper bags. My father used to hold the bag in his arm to carry it home. That made my mother even more furious, and she would say, "You see! You make people think that you buy food for your family, and what you have there may look like a lot but isn't enough for one meal."

The two ended up having a row, which made me cry every Sunday lunchtime. My father then had a siesta. When he woke up-,he took his bike and returned to the pub. At times he came home late afternoon and used the bike as a support while walking because he was too drunk to ride it. Then, before I had to go to bed, he left again to go to the pub. Then, I didn't hear him return. I have never understood why my father had money to get drunk three times on a Sunday, while I was the only child at school with a slate. A slate was just like a teacher's blackboard, only much smaller. All the other pupils in the class had exercise books. They could write and draw on white paper with colored pencils. They had a record to keep of their artwork, while I had to wipe my work of art from the slate in preparation for the next lesson, identical to what the teachers do on the black board.

One day, I had a dream that I was playing with friends and had to spend a penny. Seconds later, I woke up because my bed was wet. My mother didn't say a word about it. Then, without me knowing, she sent my brother to get a flexible bush branch. On a convenient occasion for her on the same day, she said, "Come here." I could see only one of her hands. Then she held my hand with her left hand and whipped my bottom with the branch she held in the other hand. By trying to run away, I only went in circles. My mother must have been dizzy by the time she finished, or she stopped whipping me because she got dizzy. That was the last time that I wet my bed. I grumbled at my brother for having collected the branch. My youngest brother also wet the bed some time later. He said to our mother, "I have been sweating, and the bed got wet." As he was younger than me, he got away with it.

## CHAPTER TWO

IN 1949, MY BIG BROTHER, MARIO, and a hired man, Camillo, were blowing big rocks to bits. First, they made holes in the rocks. One man was holding a hand-held drill bit, and the other one hit the bit with a sledgehammer. They took turns to hold the drill bit and use the sledgehammer. They were doing this for weeks. I simply didn't have the slightest idea of what they were doing.

I continued with what had by now become my daily routine: school, and after school, taking the animals grazing. If I was occasionally watching them making holes in the rocks, my brother would probably ask me to get some water. Now for some unknown reason, we had no tap water. To get the water, I had to go to a neighbor with a bucket and ask them if I could get water from their water pump outside their house.

One had to prime the pump with some water and start pumping. The pump was manually operated by moving a lever up and down until the water came up. At times, the pump had to be primed twice before it would function. At the opposite end of the lever, there was the pipe where the water came out. It had a hook on the pipe where the bucket could be hooked on. This way, I could fill the bucket and take it to the workers. As the water came from way below ground level, it was reasonably cool. That was a disadvantage for me because when the water in the bucket got tepid, I was told, "Fabio, get some fresh water. This in the bucket has got too warm."

After several weeks, the two workers started blowing up the rocks. I can remember having had to go indoors and then hearing an enormous bang. Then we would go and see what had happened to the rock. All I could see was that the big rock had disintegrated and had partly disappeared. Now the discussions started with the two of them. "We have used too much dynamite." "We have to try less on the next rock." The rocks were of different sizes, and they were discussing, "How much dynamite do we use for this one?"

After days of trying, I think that they got it nearly correct. The rocks didn't disappear in a thousand bits in all directions but remained crumbled up in the area where the rock had been. I still didn't know why they wanted the big rocks made smaller. After all the rocks with the handmade holes had been blown up, they started to move the smaller rocks in a wheelbarrow to a selected area, and these were piled up in a heap. The wheelbarrows were heavy and wooden and had a metal ring on the wooden wheel. This must have been a heavy and slow process.

After a while, they ended up with a four-wheel hand trailer. One person had to guide it while pulling it while the other one pushed it. It didn't take them long to realize that if two men pushed, they could load more stones on the cart. I got the job of steering it. I felt quite honored to have been able to help. It sounded good, but it wasn't that easy. The wheels were just like the one from the wheelbarrow. They all had steel rings on the external part of the wheels. So, as soon as they hit a small stone, the steering mast pulled me to one side or the other. It didn't take long before I started disliking that job.

In the spring of 1949, I discovered what all the stones blown to bits were for. My brother, Mario, started building a house. Camillo, who was now the bricklayer, set up shuttering for the construction of the walls. Then earth was taken from the base of the big excavation. The weather caused the earth to loosen from the front of the excavation cliff. The stones had a tendency to fall down and roll away some distance from the base of the excavation, while the earth simply stayed where it fell. So that was comparatively easy to shovel onto the cart. This earth was to be mixed with cement and shoveled in layers into the prepared shuttering. One layer of concrete then one layer of stones, which had been prepared over a period of months.

My job was to get water and more water. I never got a free moment to do what I liked to do. The water butts with the water for mixing cement never stayed full for long. The drinking water constantly got warm as well. What would we have done without the neighbor with the water pump? Walking from home to the neighbor and back with full buckets of water, I felt the buckets become heavier and heavier as the day passed. I didn't know why Lodovioco, Pino, and Ignaz weren't at home.

The house that was being built was nearly square. There was a corridor in the center going from front to back, with two rooms on each side of the corridor. That made three bedrooms and one kitchen-dining room, and a part of the kitchen was divided and used as a pantry. When the walls were finished, the roof was constructed. That was an event that will not be forgotten.

Lorries weren't heard of in those days. The proprietor of the local shop and pub also had a horse transport service. With the horse, they collected the roofing tiles. Somehow, the horse kicked my brother, Pino, straight in the face. He was in the hospital for a long time. He had two scars from the horseshoe for a long time.

Sand was used for the plastering. The sand was made from the earth that was taken from the face of the big excavation. To separate the small particles from the bigger ones, the earth was shoveled onto a net. The net was fixed to a wooden frame which held the edges of the net on all external parts. The net had become a sieve with holes. At the top, there were two supports fitted to make the frame stand in a vertical position. Then, when the earth was thrown at the top against the net, the fine sand passed through the sieve and accumulated at the back of the net.

This sand was the best toy Claudio and I had ever had. At times, Claudio and I were alone and had some time to play. We used to sit in the sand and form racing cars around our legs. That was just great stuff, driving these cars. Then, when Mario saw that the sand was spread out, he used to get mad at us. Yes, we got told off, but the temptation was just too great to resist. Not only that, our mother used to complain as well because we got our trousers stained.

We finally got some water laid on to the new house. We had two taps. One tap was in the kitchen over a stone sink, and the other was on the external wall for the garden and a fountain. The fountain was also used for the washing and to wash ourselves after we moved in. The best part of all this was that I didn't have to carry water any more. Had the water supply been done at the beginning, I wouldn't have had to carry water at all. I asked myself why grown-ups don't do things the right way round. First, I had to carry the heavy buckets of water for months. Then came the big event of having running water in the house.

The house was on a big plot and was built to one side of the plot. It was raised so that there were five steps to get to the front door. The rest of the land was open land with no neighbors on the village side and very few on the other side. The nearest neighbor was the one where I got the water from, and that was several minutes' walk away. As time passed, parts of land got sold by the owner until both sides next to our plot had been built on.

At the front of the plot of land was a dirt road, while at the rear was a saw mill at the base of another excavation. The main road SS12 was alongside the saw mill. On the other side of the SS12 road, there were some fruit orchards, and then came the river Adige. At some distance after the river was the railway line. It was all flat land until it got to the extreme side of this valley. Then, there were mountains with the occasional village scattered here and there up the hillside. The big excavation made the ground flat so that it could be built on. Beyond the excavation where we got the rocks from for the building, there was the forest which stretched up the hill to reach the bare cliff of the mountain Matrud.

When the land nearest the front door was sold by the owner, it was discovered that the lowest step of the entrance to the new house was, in fact, in line with the boundary. By walking off the bottom step, one ended up in the neighbor's land. This was intolerable. Therefore, it had to be changed. I fixed this mistake years later when I went there on holiday with my family. I simply reversed the steps. I built a balcony with steps at the front and rear. From the balcony to the neighbor's boundary, there was now enough space to walk in between the two.

To mark a plot of land in Italy, it gets measured, and at the corners, they make a hole for a square stone approximately

600 mm high. A part of this gets buried in the ground while the top part of the stone has a + on it. They call it the cross, and these mark one corner of the plot. These stones get moved with ease and end up causing the most terrible rows between neighbors.

Once the cornerstones are placed, an honest person sees them as a sacrosanct object to be left in place. However, others see them as something that can be moved in their favor.

We moved from the barracks to the new house before the winter. As it was all built of stone, it was colder than the wooden barracks where we had lived. We had water in the kitchen where we could wash in the mornings and before going to bed. That was when we didn't wash in the fountain. The light switches were made by my brother. The money must have been scarce, and he hand-made the light switches with a small wooden board fitted to the wall. This particular board had a wooden arm fitted to it that operated like a swivel similar to scissors. Each wooden part had a light wire fitted to it with a small nail. With the movement of closing the wooden scissors, the nails made contact, and the light functioned. By opening the scissors, the light went out.

The toilet was the old toilet we had used before. It was just a bit further to go now than before, but it was as cold as ever in the winter. In the summer, one could hardly breathe from the natural aroma. In consequence, a new toilet was built on the outside of the new house— again with a wooden platform which had one hole for the grown-ups and one for the children. The barracks was eventually auctioned, dismantled, and taken away.

## CHAPTER THREE

THIS YEAR was also the year of my first communion. I had to prepare for the catechism, and there was so much to learn by heart. As soon as I had learned one thing by heart, there was something new to learn. The learning for the catechism seemed never-ending. Then, if we didn't know the replies to the priest's questions, he could be extremely cruel and hit me with a square meter stick. Years later, a school friend said, "Have you ever noticed that the priest only hit children from the poor families? Even if at times I knew less than you, he never touched me nor others from the richer families." At the time, I was simply too young and naive to realize the priest's discriminating behavior.

Of course, I was too scared to say something at home about his behavior because the priest was always right. I would probably have been punished at home as well if I had said something. On top of that, I had to try to hide the bruises that were left on the back of my hands by the meter-long, square ruler he used. My cousin was made so nervous by this priest that his mind went totally blank as soon as the priest asked him a question. I felt sorry for him as soon as the priest said his name.

At some stage before the first communion, the bishop came to visit the class. He asked the questions and was so surprisingly nice to us. Yes, he was so nice that when he asked my cousin a few questions, my cousin knew all the replies without any hesitation. All the class was surprised by his knowledge of catechism.

The first communion was really something to look forward to, and all the class prepared for it. The school in the village was bilingual. It was a village in the Tirol, which was several kilometers from the Italian Tyrolean border. The schools in the Tirol had Italian classes with German as a second language, and vice versa. My parents chose to send me to the German school, and we had some Italian lessons every week. I found the mixture of the two languages extremely confusing. As both languages were spoken in the village by most people, I didn't really know that they were two separate languages. Then in the class, the teacher taught all subjects in German except for Italian. Then came the Italian teacher who taught just Italian. To me, she was just another teacher who confused things.

The confusion came when we learned to write the language. The Italian alphabet is shorter than the German alphabet. I didn't know that at the time. I knew that one teacher said that we had to use the *k* with some words and *ck* with some other words. Then the other teacher said that we had the *c* and *ch,* which had the same sound as a k. Then let's not forget that there is the q too to add to the confusion. I could never understand why we had to use ph instead of *f* and *q* instead of *c* or *k* or just *c.* Why should one learn so many combinations to obtain just one sound? Well, there is the *f, ph,* and *v,* which also have the same sound. It did take me ages to learn the rules, and then there were the never-ending exceptions. *Cu,* if followed by a vowel, becomes *qu.* Then, there are the exceptions, for instance, cuore, which means heart, becomes *cuore* and not *quore.*

On top of that, I had difficulties with reading. I simply could not read a word as a word. I had to read letter by letter, just like we had done the first year at school. I was given homework, and often that was to read a certain number of pages aloud. I could hardly read aloud when there were others at home. But I could do it when I was alone with my mother. On her hearing me read, she got frustrated. She took the book from me and read it fluently, just as if she was speaking it. So that was my homework done. How could grown-up, intelligent people make such a mess formulating a word? With numbers, a 1 means 1 and remains 1 unless it is changed. Then even if it is changed, it becomes a different but positive sum. It can be 11, 111, or whatever one wants it to become, and the options are endless. With ten digits, one can make an endless 100 percent positive sum with no exceptions. With letters, one can have *f, v,* and *ph* for the identical sound. In German, the *f* is pronounced as *f* as for Fabio. Then *v* is also pronounced as *f* as *v* for Vater. Wait, then we have *ph,* which sounds like *f,* like *ph* for photo.

After my homework of reading, which was done by my mother, I had to get on with some daily chores. There was a time that we were three brothers in different classes at the same time. As we had to share a book, I often had to go to my brother's class to borrow the German reading book. I can't remember having had an Italian reading book.

It was a custom to go to church before going to school in the mornings. Church at 07 hours, school at 08 hours. There were two churches in the village, the old and the new church. The new church was so new that it was extremely bare of frescoes. It had tall windows, high on the sides of the walls, with decorated glass. They must have been donated by different people from the village. At the base of each window, there was a name written on the glass.

One name is that of my grandfather. That was the father of my mother. My grandfather lived halfway up the mountain and had a farm. His grounds on the property were ever so steep. There were parts of it where, if one fell over, one just kept on rolling down the slope for some distance. Here also lived my oldest aunt. She had nine children. Eight boys and one girl.

The grounds there were mainly laid out to vineyards. There were other trees as well, like apples, apricots, cherries, pears, almonds, plums, and such like. We loved to go to my grandfather's farm when the cherries were ready to be picked by us children. We would climb up the tree to where the cherries were plentiful, then hang onto the tree with one hand and pick cherries with the other hand and stuff them into our mouths, a few at a time.

Then there was an enormous fig tree, which had big, brown, sweet figs. We also loved almonds and filled our pockets with them to take home. That wasn't allowed. My grandfather said, "You can eat as many as you like, but you can't fill your pockets and take them away."

Come to think of it, my brother and I took friends as well to my grandfather's farm. I used to really like going to my grandfather's farm. That normally happened on Sunday afternoons that I or we used to go there. With nine cousins, there was always someone to play with. We could play all sorts of games. Hide and seek was good fun. Then, jumping from the hay stack within the barn was something we all liked.

There were many chickens, a few cows, and a few cats. There was also a wine cellar where my grandfather kept his own home-made wine. All grown-ups in the village commented on how good his wine was. At that age, I didn't like wine, but I loved grape juice. The grape juice was loved by the kids for about two weeks. Then it started to ferment, and it slowly became unpleasant for me to drink.

My grandmother was a really nice lady. She took care of the chickens. She fed them and collected the eggs. There were periods that a chicken wouldn't lay her eggs in the normal nest prepared for them. She would go to a place where her eggs wouldn't be taken. Then she would sit on her eggs until the chicks would hatch. I think that everybody likes those newly born tiny, fluffy, furry balls, and their own mother loved them most of all. A mother chicken is extremely protective of her chicks.

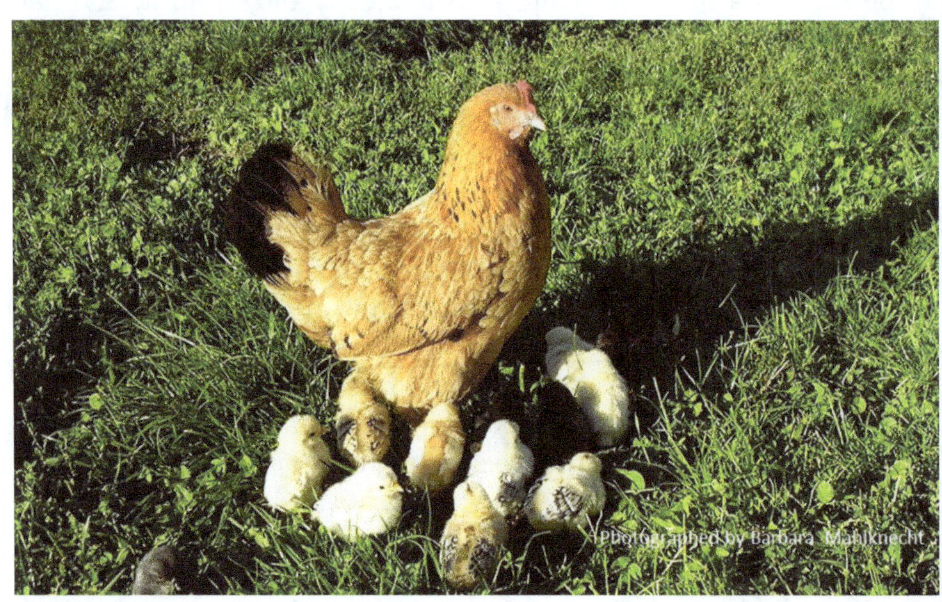
Photographed by Barbara Mahlknecht

To avoid having too many chicks, my grandmother would test to see how many chickens would have laid an egg that day. She could tell by feeling the chicken's back side if there was an egg or not. Then she would watch the chickens to see if one wandered off to where she shouldn't have gone to lay her egg. At times, my grandmother didn't have the endless time to watch a chicken before she decided to go and lay her egg.

To speed things up in this process, I learned a new trick. My grandmother sprinkled salt on the chicken's bottom. That made them lay the egg much quicker. Then she just observed and followed the chicken when she wandered off to her private nest. There, my grandmother would, at times, find many hidden eggs.

## CHAPTER FOUR

ONE OF OUR NEIGHBORS was like a grandfather to all the children and a source of information for the grown-ups. If grown-ups lacked knowledge about something, they would go to him for the info and advice. As a child, I liked going to him. His son was friends with my parents and bigger brothers, and his grandson was one year younger than me, and we were friends too.

One day this old man died, and my mother went to give her condolences to the family and had taken me with her. The grown-ups were talking and talking and saying how nice the body looked. At one point, my mother asked me to kiss the cheek of this body. I was holding back, and she repeated, "Go on, give him a kiss on his cheek." At first, I tried not to understand. After which, she got more stern. I ended up kissing that cold face on the cheek, which I absolutely detested doing. I simply could not understand how a mother could do that to a son. Kissing a cold cheek, on top of that, the cheek of a dead person, was absolutely horrendous. It sent shivers and goose pimples down my body.

Around about this time, I learned to ride a bicycle. It was a man's bike, and I had to insert one leg under the bar to reach the pedal on the other side. The son of my godmother, Diego, who was a few years older than me, held the bike, and I was pedaling. Then, when I had to brake, I said to Diego, "Stop now." He didn't stop. After I had fallen, I saw that he was way back and close to where I had started. That was my first and unforgettable ride on a bicycle.

## CHAPTER FIVE

IN LATE AUTUMN AND WINTER, the job in the field for us small boys was to collect the branches that got cut from the grapevines and fruit trees. They had to be made into bundles and tied with a flexible branch of a willow tree. These willow trees grew along ditches. The branches were long, thin, and flexible. These branches were normally collected by one of the grown-ups and were laid in water to become even more flexible. These branches were then used as string. The bundles of branches were tied with them and were also used to tie the grape branches to the pergola wires supporting them. In this area, the vine stems grew straight up for approximately one meter. Then the branches were trained on supporting wires, which were nearly in a horizontal position, that went the length of the pergola.

All the bundles of tied up branches had to be loaded on the hand-drawn cart and pulled home. Once dried, those vine branches were excellent for lighting fires in the wood burner.

The soil had to be turned on both sides of the grape plants. This was done by the grown-ups. In the spring, the boys had to clean the new shoots off the stems of the vines. The nutrition had to go into the grapes and not into the shoots. As new shoots continued to grow, they had to be constantly cleaned from the stems. Just like weeding, that was also a job that never ended until the harvest.

The best time was the harvest time. We went to the field early morning when the grass was wet from the dew. A cart with a big container was parked at one end of the field. Some others from the village came and helped with the harvest. They all cut the grapes except the children. They ended up in a container held in one hand, something like a bowl with a handle on it. When that was filled, it got emptied into a bigger container. One person would carry that bigger container on their back to the big container on the cart. The children had to trample the grapes in the container to get them squashed, to make more room in the round container.

And yes, we could eat grapes at will. After I had eaten a few bunches of grapes, I had enough and would only choose the occasional grape that had a particular attraction. Either it was bigger or darker in color, or it simply stood out in some way that caught my attention. It was normally sunny when we harvested the grapes. When evening came, and it was time to go home, we children had sticky legs from the grape juice. Walking home barefoot, we could feel the warm asphalt of the street. This was the main street that was in the Adige Valley. The asphalt was so warm that we laid on it with our sticky arms and legs. At that time, we could hear a car coming from a long way off. Apart from that, cars driving by were extremely rare. Some days we saw a car, and some days we didn't see one. Pino, Ignaz, Klaus, and I all lay in the street to soak in the warmth of the warm asphalt during the dusk. Once the sun went behind the mountains, it soon got dark. The lights of a car could be seen in the distance long before it could be heard.

We got home and received some supper. At times, supper was prepared with leftovers from lunchtime. Then after eating, we were all tired and went to bed. Soon after that, Mother made us all get up, and we had to go in the external fountain to wash our bodies from the sticky mess that was on us from the grape trampling. We were just a bunch of children with sticky arms and legs from the grape juice. The bedding had to be washed by hand; therefore, it was understandable that she couldn't let a bunch of kids go to bed dirty as we were. Actually, we liked going in the fountain at this time of day. The water got warmed by the sun during the day to become pleasantly warm. Then, it cooled off during the night to become bitterly cold by the morning.

As we didn't have many grape vines, this grape harvesting only lasted two days. After this harvest, the daily routine continued as always. Normally, at harvest time, the school had already started the new school year. That normally started in September, while the grape harvesting was done during September, October. The families with land were allowed to keep the children absent from school so that they could help with the harvest. Children received time off school for the harvest period and not just to help at home; therefore we helped other land owners as well. When needed, this was also done all throughout the summer.

One of the first fruits to be picked were cherries. Then in June and July came the early pears. There was one farmer that used only children to collect this type of pears. They were small pears, and it took some doing to fill a box. We got paid for doing this job. So much per box filled, but the boxes had to be full. The other children told me that if the boxes are not full, the farmer will deduct from the price he pays per box. In such a case, it was better to overfill the boxes. Only, when we placed a new empty box one on top of the filled one, I had to take some pears off the box because it was too full to place the next box on top. The top of the corners of the boxes were slightly higher than the rest of the box. That was deliberate so that the new box would rest on the corners of the box and not damage the fruit.

The fruit was delicate and couldn't be bruised. In fact, I was shown how to handle it with care, how to pick the fruit, how to place it in the sack, and how to empty the sack into the box. I had the sack hanging on a strut over my shoulder, and it hung on my side with the opening at my waist level. The fruit had to be laid gently in the sack. It had to be deposited gently on top of the fruit that was already in the sack. If the fruit was dropped on top of other fruit, it would have been bruised and would have shown a bruise mark. This had to be avoided at all costs, I was told. At the end of each day, each one of the boys would calculate how many boxes each one had filled and how much had been earned.

Once this harvesting was finished, I went to the farmer to be paid. "Ah, don't be so hasty," he replied. "I haven't been paid myself yet, and you will have to wait until I get paid." In the autumn, I heard that some of the other boys had been paid. I went back to the farmer and asked for my money. Yes! Now it sounded more promising. The farmer was sitting at a table. He looked for a list on the table and said, "Oh yes, I see that you picked so many boxes of pears." "Yes, that is correct," I replied. "You see," he then said, "your boxes weren't filled; therefore, I have to deduct a part from the price." My arguments that it wasn't so didn't help in the least. I ended up receiving two-thirds of what I should have received. At that point, I promised myself never to work for that man again. This man lived near the new village church. Some years later, I heard that he had jumped from the bell tower to his death.

## CHAPTER SIX

THE WINTER CAME, and we always had snow covering the countryside. Skis were only for the richer families and were mainly used as a form of transportation. One could say, "I use the skis instead of a bike." At home, we had a sledge which I liked to use. The only problem was that the slopes were short. There were places where the slopes were longer, and the snow was compact. That was much more fun than sledging on short slopes with soft snow.

Close to the school and church, there was a slope that the children used to go sliding on. They took a run from a few meters back towards the slope and slid down the slope standing up. To make it function better, we poured water down the slope and along the flat part on the base of the slope. When that froze, we slid a lot farther. This very same slope was used by the grown-ups to go to church. The children used the side of the slope to walk up it. We had also made some steps in the snow for us to walk up it. But for the grown-ups, it was too dangerous, and they constantly sprayed ashes on our ice track. This watering and ash spraying continued throughout the winter, and the boys constantly used it during the school breaks throughout the winter.

The school hours were from 8 till 10. After, we had a short break. At midday, we had an hour-long break. The break might have been one hour and thirty minutes. It was long enough to walk home, have lunch, and return to school. My cousins lived farthest from the school, and it must have taken them twenty minutes to half an hour to walk just one way. Then we had two hours of lessons, a short break, and the school then finished at five in the afternoon.

Christmas time was just great. All the family was together, and we had a Christmas tree and a big Crèche under it. Pino was the one who was most interested in preparing the tree and Crèche. On Christmas night, the boys had to go to bed early because the baby

Jesus couldn't bring the presents if the boys were still up. Yes, the baby Jesus brought the presents overnight. He only came if we had gone to bed. The boys slept three in one room in a double bed, and three in another room in a double bed. My father slept alone in one room, and my mother slept on the sofa in the kitchen-dining room.

From baby Jesus, I received a brand new pair of shoes. I was delighted when I opened my parcel. I often received hand-me-downs, what my brothers had used. But this time, I had my own new shoes. I tried and tried to get them on. I was really looking forward to showing my friends my new shoes when I went to church. Christmas day was just like a Sunday, and we all went to church. In the end, it became time to go to church, and I had to go wearing my old shoes because the new shoes were simply too small. I also received some coloring pencils. I was looking forward to trying the new colored pencils. I only had my slate to draw on. I drew on it, and then I simply couldn't wipe it off. Then the chalk wouldn't write on the coloring. My slate was ruined. Now I was forced to ask my father for the money to buy a writing book. At last, I got my very own exercise book. I was the last in my class to have used a slate.

## CHAPTER SEVEN

LATE SPRING OF 1950, I was told that I would go "Ai Freschi." I can't find a word for that expression in English. It is an expression that the Italians use for a place that is high up in altitude, and where the temperature in the summer is fresher-cooler than it is in the base of the valleys. I knew from hearsay that it was a summer camp or a place where only the rich could afford to have their vacations. But there were youth groups as well that used to go to such places. I used to hear about it, but I didn't know anybody who had been to such a place. That was what I imagined being at a summer school would have been. To go "Ai Freschi" was only for the privileged. Now I would be going there myself. How nice! I was really looking forward to it.

One day, my mother, Pino, and I left with a rucksack that had some of my clothing in it. We walked to the Magre train station and went by train to Bronzol. That was the third stop after we got on the train. It was ever so exciting; this was the first time that I had gone by train. We got off the train in Branzol and walked in the direction of the village. We walked through the village and started to walk up a stone road that was lined with trees and bushes. This road was just like the road that went to my grandfather's farm.

They had used stones to line the base of the road. To transport goods on these roads, wagons were used. At the front, they had wheels for the summer and a sledge for the winter. Then from the wheels or sledge, there were tree trunks attached to them. The back of the trunks rested on the road. This made the load more level going down those steep roads. Then the load was placed on the tree trunks. To go downhill with a heavy load, a brake was used. At the back of the trunks, a chain was fitted to each trunk. The chain went under the trunk and was squashed between the trunk and the stones of the road. With the constant use of the chains, the stones got worn and formed a channel on each side of this road.

The three of us just walked and walked up this road until we got to a village called Aldagno. The walk continued toward Pietralba. Pietralba was a famous pilgrimage place. For me, that was the only pilgrimage place that I knew of. We were about halfway between Aldagno and Pietralba when we turned left and walked to a farm house. A big gate had to be opened to enter a big yard. Once in the yard, there was a big stable and barn on the left and the farm house on the right. There, we were met by a strange lady. The grown-ups started talking in a German dialect, and I wasn't really listening and didn't really know why we stopped there. We were given something to eat there, after which my mother and Pino continued their walk to Pietralba. I was asked to stay there, and they would return.

The lady took me to a room on the ground floor and showed me a bed and also showed me which drawer I could use for my clothing. Then I was taken to the stable, which was full of cows, and there were four horses too. I was feeling a bit strange. I didn't know what was happening. I was with this strange person, and why was she showing me the stables? Then I was left to myself until my mother and Pino returned. Thank goodness that they returned. But I still had the uncertainty about what was happening. I was thinking. "Why was I shown where to keep my clothing, and why was I shown the stable?" After a while, I was abandoned to my destiny by my family. They left to go home and left me there, abandoned in the hands of strangers; Ai Freschi! I couldn't feel the difference in the temperature between there and home.

During the evening meal, there were what appeared to be many people. They appeared to be many probably because they were all strangers to me. There were three men of different ages, and one boy who was just a few years older than me. Then there were three ladies. One of them was the lady who had shown me my room. After the evening meal, the evening prayer was celebrated, after which I went to bed and then realized that I was, in fact, abandoned a long way from home. I was missing my brothers, cousins, and friends. I started crying and eventually went to sleep.

Then what seemed to be the middle of the night, I got woken up. I was given the time to get my trousers and a shirt on, then I was taken barefooted to the stable and was shown how to groom the animals. In one hand, I had to hold a scraper with four blades that were rugged, and in the other hand, I had an oval-shaped brush. With those tools, I had to groom the cows. The horses were too high for me. I simply couldn't reach their top part. But the cows absolutely loved being pampered. To be scratched behind their horns on the head, they couldn't get enough of that. That was best done with the fingernails. That was a spot where they couldn't scratch themselves, and they loved me to do it.

Some grown-ups were milking during this period, and others were cleaning the stable and preparing the bedding for the cows. At seven, we had breakfast. Then after breakfast, one of the men showed me what to do. He gave me a whip and took me to the stable. What a whip! I had never used one before. Now I had to learn how to use it. At the stable, with some help from others that were there, the chains were removed from the cows' and horses' necks, and they were guided out into the yard. Every cow had a bell with a specific tune which identified each cow. The horses had nothing on their necks once they were let loose. The chains were simply laid in the manger, to be re-used when the cows returned. Above the manger, there was the name of each cow, written in chalk on a board.

In the yard, there was a water trough where all the cows went to have a drink. Then the big gate got opened, and all the cows were guided along this private way to the stone road we had come on the day before. On this road, the cows knew where to go all by themselves. They turned left and then went into a forest on the right. In this forest, they started grazing. The cows were left to themselves as this man showed me the big area where the cows could graze. All the area had a fence with vertical wooden posts and three horizontal wooden posts fixed to them. Then, he explained to me when I had to guide the cows back home for lunchtime.

From where we were, the church bells from Aldagno could

be heard, and when I would hear them at lunchtime, I had to take the cows back. He gave me some bread and cheese for my morning break before leaving me to it. Once he left, I had a look at my brunch in the bag. There was a chunk of homemade bread and the biggest piece of homemade cheese that I had ever had to myself.

The grazing land was surrounded by forest and had a big grass field in it. The cows had their heads down and were eating grass. They slowly walked while eating to the end of the field, then they turned all by themselves and started grazing in the opposite direction. They separated a bit between one another, but they all stayed in the big field. When I was hungry, I sat on the base of a tree that had been cut and ate my bread and cheese. I truly liked that bread and cheese I received for my break, and it was plentiful. What I didn't like was the fact that I had to carry it around with me until I had my break.

I had to practice using the whip. I knew that by flipping the cord of the whip, it would make a bang that should have scared the animals to move away from it. I practiced and practiced. I lost count of the number of times I received the whip round my ears. It wasn't as easy as I had thought. It was something that I would not have learned to do in one day. Eventually, I heard the church bells, and I started gathering the animals and guided them to the exit of this pasture and back to the farm. All the cows knew what they had to do. I basically had to follow them and make sure I hadn't left one behind.

Some cows stopped to have a drink from the fountain in the big yard. Some drank from the fountain, while others drank from the constant running water that came from an open-ended pipe with no tap. Other cows went directly to the stable and to their own place. They knew exactly where they had to go, and the horses did as well. I knew that each cow had its name above its place, but they couldn't read. So how did they know which place to go to when there were forty places to choose from? Once they were all chained up again, we went for lunch.

We had dumplings for lunch. Dumpling were made of

a paste of flour, bread crumbs, seasoning, speck (which is smoked bacon) cut in small cubes, eggs, and salt. This paste was made into balls the size of a tennis ball and then boiled in water. Then they were served with a salad. The prayer giving thanks was celebrated before every meal.

Rose was the lady who showed me my room the day before. After lunch, Rose asked me to follow her. She walked to the vegetable garden and asked me to remove the weeds from the vegetable beds between now and the time I had to take the cows back to the pasture. Honestly, that was a slow job, as the garden was big. With a bit of luck, I would have finished it in a week or so. After I had been pulling weeds for an hour or so, I was asked to take the animals back to the pasture. The church bells didn't ring in the afternoon. I was shown where the sun had to be before I returned with the herd.

From the pasture, I could see the top of the mountains, which were on the other side of the Adige valley. I wanted to look down those mountains as much as possible to see if I could see my village. I climbed up on trees to see if I could see a bit farther down those mountains. No such luck. There was no tree tall enough that would have given me that view. I also had to practice using the whip, and bit by bit, it started making the *bang* noise that I wanted from it. Yes! Now it looked as if I could succeed in mastering the whip.

The herd knew better than me when it was time to return to the stable. They walked by themselves, while still grazing, toward the exit of the pasture. Then when I looked at the sun, I could see that it was about where it should have been. Once back in the stable, they had to be milked. I was too small to milk. Instead of milking, I helped to finish spreading the bedding on the floor for the animals. When the milking was finished, we went to have our supper. After dinner and prayers, I helped with the cream separation. Some of the milk was used for our own consumption, and the cream was taken from the milk with a special machine. This machine had one big container where the whole milk was poured into. Then it had two outlets, one for the skimmed milk and one for the cream.

To achieve the separation, a handle had to be turned on the separator with a constant rhythm.

When this was finished, I could go to bed to cry because of my homesickness. This was my first day's work, and it became my normal routine, except on Sundays. On Sundays after breakfast, I would go to the fountain, which had constant running water, and wash my face. After we finished in the stable, we had breakfast. Then I got dressed up in my Sunday clothing. Later in the morning, we went to church. For these occasions, I wore my shoes. At times, I was taken to Aldagno church, and at times, to Pietralba Sanctuary. I have never asked why this was. I simply went where I was taken. Along the Pietralba way, there was the "Via Crucis" crucifixion stations. After the mass, we returned to the farm and had lunch.

After lunch, I had the afternoon to myself. I could do what I liked. What can one do if one is all by one's self? I had no one to play with. In the hay barn, there was some hay from the previous year. Jumping off the hay stack is fun if one can do it with friends. The youngest son, Toni, was a few years older than me and did his own things. Toni had two brothers, Luis and Sepel. Then, he had two sisters, Rose and Anna. Toni had an aunt as well, and she was called Nondel. She wouldn't speak to anyone; she spoke to herself, and smiled and laughed to herself as well. She helped mainly in the stable.

## CHAPTER EIGHT

TONI'S PARENTS were also there. His father was always at the table at meal times. Apart from that, I didn't see him much. Toni's mother must have become mentally ill at some stage of her life. She didn't work in any way. Rose would guide her to where Rose wanted her to be. At times, the mother would show some resistance, but she normally gave in to Rose's insistence. She was often in the fields and returned with a hand full of field flowers or herbs, or whatever she found of interest, I imagine. I never did discover what she did with her precious collections. She used to talk to herself as well, but she didn't smile or laugh like Nondel did.

There was a lady in Laghetti who was just like this lady. She lived in "La Casa Grande," the big house. Hearsay would have it that this lady had a room full of herbs, and I never heard this lady speak.

The Sunday afternoon slowly passed, and the slight boredom made me think of home and of my friends more than when I was busy. When I went to bed, I still shed the odd tear. Monday repeated itself just like the previous Monday and every day after that, too. On Mondays, I would wear clean clothing for the week. The weeding I had to do after lunch, I finished during the week. Great, I thought. I didn't like weeding that much. Then when I said to Rose that I had finished, she took me back to the garden and made me start from the beginning. New weeds had grown, but they were still small, a lot smaller than the ones I had pulled out. At that point, I realized that I would never finish weeding. By the time I got to the end of weeding the vegetable beds, I had to start from the beginning. After this weeding, I had to guide the herd to the pasture just like the previous week.

In the pasture, I heard an unusual noise. It was like *grrrrrr-raw, grrrrrrrraw, aeeeeeeee, aeeeeeeeee.* I started walking in the direction from where it had come. I went beyond the fence from the pasture, and I simply could not see anything that could have caused it. I heard this same noise on and off at irregular times. The herd was simply grazing without noticing that I wasn't present. For a few days, I walked in the direction of where that noise had come from. I waited there for a while to see if I could see what made that noise. After I had gone there several times, I heard the noise much closer. It wasn't close enough for me to see what had caused it. The next time, I had to wait a bit farther along the forest.

One day, I finally discovered what caused that noise. It was a big, beautiful, male peacock. This was the first time that I had seen a live peacock. I was pleased to have finally discovered what made that noise and was even more pleased to have seen a peacock for the very first time. When I returned to the farm, I was tempted to tell them. Then I realized that by telling them, they would have known that I had gone beyond the pasture boundaries. Therefore, I kept the wonderful news to myself.

I had started to copy the noises the birds and animals made. I had also learned to tell what noise it was. For instance, when a cow was separated from her calf that was only a few days old, she would make a distinct misery noise. When birds had some animal threatening their nest, they would also make a distressful noise and did everything possible to draw the danger away from the nest. At times, the horses got separated from one another in the pasture. Then one would make a calling noise, and one of the others would probably reply. I practiced copying those animal noises until I got good at it.

One night, a cow had a lovely little calf that I could easily have become friends with. For the next few days, the mum's milk was just for her baby. It was a special milk that couldn't be mixed with the rest of the milk. When the mother had to abandon her baby to go to the pasture, she cried just like I did when I was led away from home. The first few days, she would bellow on and off, but she would also try to get to the stable where her baby was. I didn't expect her to escape from the pasture and go back to the stable, but she did. When she got to the stable, the stable door was closed, and she had to stay outside. I had to get her back to the pasture. After this, I waited close by the exit of the pasture. Now when she would try to leave the pasture, I had to stop her. This was the only exit from the pasture, and I would see her coming.

Just as I thought, it didn't take long before she came to the exit to go to her calf. Over the days, her attempts to leave the pasture got less and less, and on the fourth day, she didn't try at all. At that time, I never understood why the calves couldn't go to the pasture with their mothers. The calves had to be weaned, and the sooner that was done, the better it was.

It was Nondel's job to train the calves to feed from a bottle and, consequently, from a bucket. She first placed her middle finger in the calf's mouth, and it would suck on her finger. Then, she slowly moved her finger into a bucket with milk, and the calf would slowly start to suck the milk with the finger still in its mouth. After this, the calf was kept separated from his mother for good. Despite not being together with his mother, he had loads of company with calves that were a bit older than him, and soon, there would be some newcomers to keep him company.

The enclosure for the calves was always good to see. As soon as I got close to the enclosure, some of the calves came close to me to sniff me and lick me. The next time a cow who just had a calf went to the pasture, for the first few days after it was separated from its baby, I waited by the exit to prevent the cow from leaving the pasture like the first one did. After a few days, they did stop trying to leave, and I could return to my normal routine.

## CHAPTER NINE

I WOULD HAVE LOVED to have seen a foal, but the mares didn't give birth while I was staying there. What was curious to see was that many cows would go to the calves' enclosure and look at the calves in it. The behavior of these animals was, at times, astonishingly human-like. With a new baby, all ladies want to see it. The cows were just the same. If a human had an itch, he would scratch himself. The cows did the same. They scratched themselves in various ways. They would often rub their neck up and down on a tree. They would also use a rear leg to scratch parts of their body, and the tongue was also used. The tail was mainly used to keep the flies away. On rare occasions, a cow would try to rub her neck on my legs and body. I wasn't sturdy like a tree, and I got simply pushed away. One cow even learned to place one of her feet gently on my foot to keep it in place while she tried to scratch her neck. At times, one would look at me and make a long hhhhmmmmmmmmmmmmm noise. What that gentle noise meant, I didn't know. I was left wondering what she wanted to say to me.

After a while, I became one of them. I was probably their shepherd or their boss. I had to be there, but I certainly wasn't needed. At times, I had the feeling that it was them that were keeping me company, rather than me being there to take care of them. Occasionally, one cow would lick another cow for a considerable length of time. It looked to me as if it was some sign of affection, which was being shown by the licking cow.

..............................................................

One day, when I was guiding the herd from the pasture to the farm, the horses, on exiting the pasture gate, turned in the opposite of the usual direction. They went toward Pietralba. I knew that I couldn't run after them and overtake them on the road. They would have simply run in front of me forever. Therefore, I went back into the pasture and ran in the forest parallel to the road where the horses were walking. A long way later, I went into the road and saw that the horses were, in fact, coming toward me. I tried making gestures with my hands and whip to make them turn round. That didn't help in the least. The horses walked past me as if I didn't exist. I had no choice but to let them go and go back to the herd. By the time I got back, the herd was waiting for me to open the gate to the farmyard. How could I now tell Luis or Sepel what had happened? How could I tell them that I lost four horses?

Luis was an understanding person, and I did like him. As I have seen him first, I told him about having lost the horses. He knew where the horses had gone to. Somewhere, there were the Alps, and there the grass is much better. Now the young men prepared a modification to the entrance of the pasture. There was some distance from the road to the pasture area. Here from the fence to the road, they erected a fence to make the turn to the right when exiting the pasture much narrower, and this fence was erected in the direction towards the farm.

A few days later, Luis and Sepel went to get the horses. Once the horses were back, they walked to the pasture with the herd. One of the sons would stand in the road, just where the opening had been narrowed, to stop the horses from walking past the entrance to the pasture. This system functioned, and it was repeated for a few days. After that, I had no more problems with losing animals.

To pass the time while I was with the herd, I looked for wild strawberries. They were small but had an outstanding flavor. At times, I filled my hand with these wild strawberries and ate them a mouthful at a time. At that moment, I thought that there wasn't anything better tasting than this wild delicacy. I also carved things on tree barks. Wood was too hard to be carved with the pen knife I had. Toni lent me his penknife so that I could do some carving on pieces of tree bark or wood.

When I looked for the peacock, I had seen a tiny quarry with slate. From there, I could lever off pieces of slate and carve them into shapes. This wasn't good for the penknife. It got blunt very quickly. There was a round sharpening stone in a workshop.

This tool had to be operated with one hand by turning a handle fixed to the stone wheel, which had its base in water. By turning the wheel, the stone was constantly wet and functioned well. For me, to turn the wheel and sharpen the knife wasn't that easy. I could see that I was no expert in sharpening knifes. I simply couldn't obtain a nice sharp blade on this penknife. Later, I used the knife blade to lever a piece of slate, and the tip of the blade broke. Now I was thinking what I could say to Toni. I ended up using the grinding stone to get a point back on the blade.

When Toni wanted his knife back to do something, he noticed what I had done. For a week, he wouldn't lend it to me— as punishment, I assumed. Before lending it to me again, he sharpened it better than I could have done, but I had to turn the wheel of the grinder for him. At least with the knife, I found something to do in the pasture. As far as the animals were concerned, I needn't have been there. I was only needed to take them to the pasture and bring them back.

One day, Anna asked me to have a look to see what the time was. They had a wall-hung chiming clock. I had to say to Anna that I didn't know how to read the time. She then showed me and explained that the small hand gave the time of the hours and the big hand gave the time of the minutes. The hours were twelve, and the minutes were sixty, and that was how I learned to tell the time.

One morning when I got up, I went to see what the time was. It was five o'clock. Now I also knew at what time I was getting up in the mornings. That was why when I was woken the first morning, it felt like it was the middle of the night.

At home, we didn't have a clock. There must have been an alarm clock and would only have been used as such. In the daytime, the time was read on shadows on the mountain. The sounding church bells were another indication of the time. The bells rang in the mornings before the early mass, at lunchtime, and again in the evening. On Sundays, the bells were rung for the big mass as well. On this rest day, the men were dressed up, and on most of them, I could see the chain of a pocket watch. Most villagers had worn a costume of their village, consisting of a three-piece suit and decorated hat. The vast majority had some sort of decoration on the left side of the hat. Some had something that looked similar to a shaving brush without the handle and was flat instead of being round. Others had feathers from different birds. Most of them had grouse feathers. During the summer, some men used carnations instead of feathers as decoration.

The ladies were dressed up too. They, too, had a costume with a long dress that nearly touched the ground and a top part that was elegant, with a white long-sleeved blouse under the top of the dress.

The farm grounds were partly on the flat and partly on sloping ground. On one side of the farmhouse, it was flat. This was mainly planted with corn. One area, small in comparison to the big field, had poppies. Big, colorful poppies with big seed pods. Once the petals had fallen, the pods would slowly change from green to brown. Once they were brown, the seeds would become ripe and loosen inside the pods. The boys showed me that I could remove the pod from the stem, open the top of the pod, and pour the seeds into my mouth.

Really, the poppies were grown for the seeds, and they were used as a filling in a sweet. The seeds were made into a paste, and then the paste was spread on a sheet of pastry of 6 to 7 cm. Then another layer of thin pastry was laid over the top of the poppy paste and was then cut into squares with a zigzag wheel. They were deep fried. Eating them was a real treat.

Down along one side of the poppy and corn fields, on the left side, if one looked at it from the farmyard, there was a long section of grass that was flat and variable in width of about 10 m. One Sunday afternoon, I think that Luis and Sepel realized that I felt lonely and had some fun with me. They took a horse from the stable and led it to this long strip of low green grass. Luis grabbed me by one arm with one hand and by my trousers with his other hand and flung me on the bare back of the horse. Then he said, "Hold yourself," and gave the horse a slap on his behind. The horse started running along this long strip of land. I had embraced the horse at the top of his neck. That didn't give me a good grip, and I slowly slid to one side and eventually fell off the horse without hurting myself. Then I had to get the horse and guide it back to Luis.

He did the same again, and this time, he said, "Hold yourself on the horse's crest hair." I did just that, and it went a lot better. I was partly cautious not to hurt the horse, and I didn't hold myself too tightly on his crest and eventually fell as well.

On another Sunday, he let me shoot with his shot gun. He set up a target at some distance away and said, "Here is the gun. You have to hold it tight to your shoulder, then aim at the target and pull the first trigger." The gun was a double barrel 12 bore shotgun and had two triggers. After the shot, Luis collected the target and showed me that it was full of small holes. He said that it was a good shot.

On another day, to have some fun over me, Luis asked me to take a hay wagon down the slopes to a specific field. This field was down a slope behind the barn. This wagon had wheels on the front and bare wooden trunks on the rear. In front of the wheels, it had a center pole where there would normally be a horse on each side of it. Towards the front, it had two wooden pins used to hold the harness. The pins slid up and down and were held in the holes by their weight. On this occasion, as I was taking this empty hay cart down the steep slopes, I was too small to control it. It simply went faster and faster.

In desperation, I lowered the rudder to the ground and put my weight on it. Fortunately, the two wooden pins at the front of the rudder served as a brake. With my weight on the rudder, they dug into the ground and slowly stopped the wagon. Now I could slowly take the wagon to where the ground was flat. The mark where the grass and soil got torn by the pins remained all summer. When I got back to the young men, they couldn't believe that I managed to take that wagon down the slope by myself. I simply couldn't think why they should have wanted a damaged wagon.

## CHAPTER TEN

AT TIMES, ROSE HAD NEW JOBS FOR ME. She gave me the job of turning the handle of the butter churn, which was filled with cream. This was the first time that I was involved with making butter. She explained that I had to turn the handle in a constant motion. It sounded like fun. I turned and turned that handle until my arm ached. Then I asked Rose how long I would have to turn it for. She replied, "You will be able to tell when the cream turns into butter." It appeared to take ages before I noticed a difference in the rhythm of being able to turn the wheel. As the butter formed, the lumps stuck to the blades of the churn and interrupted the rhythm of the turning handle.

The butter was then taken out by Rose and kneaded to remove the buttermilk. Then she filled a wooden butter mold, which had an edelweiss carving in the base of it. When Rose was finished with pressing the butter in this mold, she would turn it round to make the butter come out of the mold. Now it was a solid block of butter with an edelweiss on top of it.

When the poppies were harvested, Rose gave me the job of making a paste from the poppy seeds. She gave me a bras pestle and mortar and showed me how to do it. There couldn't be anything simpler than making this paste. One had to take a measure, fill it with poppy seeds, empty the seeds into the brass container, and stamp them. This, too, took ages of stamping before it became a paste. Then the paste was removed from the container, and the process continued with the next load. I never discovered how the poppy pods were opened to remove the seeds from them. To open a pod for a mouth full of seeds was one thing. To open them by the thousand, well, they should have had some tool to do it with.

Tree sap was collected by Luis and Sepel. There were larch trees in the forest. Some of them had a hole drilled in them. In the hole, there was a small channel inserted where the sap came out from the tree and dripped into a container which was fitted just in the right place. The containers filled with tree sap were taken to the farm and replaced with new ones. I never did discover what happened to the tree sap.

One day in the pasture, I found what looked like a wasp nest in the ground. These creatures were several times bigger than the normal wasps. I reported it to the boys. Sepel put on the protective clothing he used to work with bees and destroyed the nest and eliminated the wasps; I didn't see them after that. They said that a person could die with just one sting from such a beast.

The corn harvesting time was getting closer. For this year's harvesting, they got a new machine. It was so big that they got two more horses for the day of collecting it. The wagon was pulled with six horses. Normally when the carts went downhill, the wheels from the rear of the wagon were removed. But to pull something uphill, they fitted wheels to the rear. Wedge-like blocks were then hanging on the rear of the cart, which were used as stops and fitted behind the rear wheels so that the horses could rest for a while. This machine would do the threshing. I had never seen threshing done before. It made a lot of dust as it separated the wheat from the ears. This machine did the separation of the grain from the ears and separated the grains from the straw as well.

One day, I was asked not to take the herd to the pasture. Down a slope to the left of the main entrance and beyond the farmyard, there were three fields with different sorts of vegetation growing in them. They told me to keep the herd on the center field of the three. That had clover growing in it, which had been cut and had partially re-grown. That could be eaten by the animals, but they couldn't eat from the other two fields. All around and in between the fields, there was grass. The clover field was big, and the first day I had no problem keeping the herd in that field. Then on the second day, it was more difficult to keep them within the clover field. I had to constantly run from field one to field three to get the cows out of there and back to field two.

On the third day, it became just impossible to keep them out of the forbidden field. I had to run to field one and get the animals back to field two. I got them back to part of field two, and then I run to field three and got them back from that field to field two. By the time I had done that, a part of the herd was back into field one. I felt that the two young men, Luis and Sepel, were watching me from somewhere and were having a good laugh watching me. The cows weren't in the least interested in the grass all around the clover field.

Then, as luck would have it, on the fourth day, I was told to take them to the prairie. That was a tremendous relief to go back to the old routine. As I didn't like to carry my bread with me, I had found a hiding place for my brunch. There was a horizontal excavation, and at the end, there was a high cliff. There were holes in this cliff, big enough for my brunch to be placed in it. That way, I didn't have to carry it with me until break time. Hiding my brunch in this hole didn't last for long. The brunch consisted most often of bread and cheese. The time came that my brunch disappeared. That was strange. How could that have happened, I asked myself. Then on the next day, it happened again.

My suspicions didn't give me peace, and I placed my brunch there for the third day. I watched from the distance to see who it was that took my brunch. It was one of the cows. By the time I ran to the hiding place to save my brunch, it was finished. A brunch that took me about ten minutes to eat, the cow grabbed the whole bag in one go, and there was nothing to be saved. I was surprised to see how far her tongue could reach into that hole to grab my bag. That convinced me that I had to find a safer place for my snack or just keep it on me.

The fields that had been harvested were empty of grain and clover and were freshly plowed. In some fields, they also sowed a specific grain to grow the following year. The mornings and evenings were getting colder and darker. The sun took longer to come up from behind the mountains and would go down sooner behind the mountains on the other side of the valley. By now, I was settled in with this family, and I had become nearly like one of them. I felt as if I was treated like a son by the father and nearly like a brother by the sons and daughters. I felt as if I was nearly one of the family. I didn't see Toni that much, and I didn't know why he was at home so rarely. I hadn't been homesick for a long time. My nostalgia for home had lasted for about two weeks.

But unexpectedly, Mario and Lodovico had come one day— I thought it was just to visit me. They had lunch with us. After lunch, the father of Luis sat with my brothers at the table and had some money in his hand. That made me think of the occasions when some strangers were there at that table, just like my brothers now, but then, he had loads of money. I never had my own money, and I didn't know the value of it. When I got some things from the local shop at home, it was recorded in the book. I could remember having seen some coins and also some small paper notes. But they didn't mean much to me. This money he had on the table was really big and had to be folded several times to fit into a big side pocket wallet. Now my brothers were given some of these big notes. Then they told me to get my clothing, and we would go home.

Now we went back the way I had come with my mother and Pino. It was so different walking the opposite of the way I had come. On the way up the road, the plantation was so fresh and green. While now, the leaves looked tired and ready to turn their colors to yellow and brown. It was nice to return home, but it was so unexpected, and I didn't know for how long I would be going home for. At home, there was my younger brother, Claudio, and my mother. Ignaz and Pino weren't there. Coming home was so joyful, but once I got home, it was something of an anti-climax.

A simple hello from my mother. There was no embrace nor sign of joy of having the abandoned son at home again. I asked her where Pino and Ignaz were. She did answer, but after her reply, I didn't understand it any better than before I had asked.

Pino did come home. He had become an apprentice in plumbing and metalworking.

## CHAPTER ELEVEN

I GOT HOME IN TIME TO CELEBRATE my eighth birthday. After this weekend, the time had come to go to school again. I was weeks late returning to school. The rest of the class was way ahead of me with the lessons. In the spring, I had left before the school closed for the summer, and I returned weeks after the classes had started.

There was also a new lady teacher that taught in my class. It didn't take her long to realize that I was way behind the others. I felt that she did more for me than she did for the others. She gave me more homework than she gave the others in the class. Even the homework became difficult to do.

My mother worked in the daytime. When she came home, she would prepare supper. After that, she did a lot of knitting. At times, when I got up in the night, she was still up knitting. She made herself strong coffee to stay awake. So, I got the job of doing the washing up and looking after the three animals that were there, plus some chickens. Wood had to be chopped for the daily use. There was a wood-burning stove that was used for the cooking, warm water, and heating. Only the kitchen-dining room had a form of heating. The wood-burning stove had an oven and a water container in which water got heated. That was the only warm water there was. For washing the dishes, it was great. At night, the fire went out, and the water got cold. In the mornings, the water took too long to get warm for it to be used for washing ourselves. So, for a daily wash, cold water was used. A portable bathtub was used for a better wash, and additional water was heated on the stove for those rare occasions.

At this time of year, in the garden, there was only winter salad left, which had to be covered thickly with straw to protect it from the frost. After that, it was collected as needed. When collecting this winter salad, I could see a mouse's nest. It used the protection of the straw to keep warm during the winter.

My christening godparents lived close to my home. My godmother would, on occasions, ask me to bring some shopping back to her after school. In return, she gave me some oranges and biscuits on the Saint Nicolas day in December. That was the first time that I had received an orange. It was so precious to me that I simply wanted to keep it so that I could feel and smell an orange.

Christmas was getting closer, and the tree and Crèche had to be prepared. In those days, I had never seen a tree being sold. We didn't have the local street market, and the local shop didn't have them for sale. Pino and I, early on a Sunday morning, went a long way up the mountain to the pine tree forest. When we got to the forest, we had something to eat and drink. It was like a nice forest picnic, similar to the breaks I had when I looked after the herd. It was nice to be in my brother's company instead of having just cows around me. We started looking for a tree in this forest. Well, it couldn't be any tree; it had to be a good balanced pine that we had to find. Then we had to find it in a place where there was a mass of trees. It had to be a place where eventually they would have been thinned out, and one tree wouldn't have been missed. Pino found just what he was looking for. He cut the tree, and we started to walk home with it.

On the way back, we heard a car in the distance. There was only one stone paved road wide enough for a horse-drawn cart and was lined on both sides by a natural dry-stone wall. The car could only come our direction, and it was forbidden to take trees.

Pino hid the tree behind some bushes behind the stone wall. Then, we walked away from the tree and back toward where we had come from. As the car eventually came, it was a two-seater FIAT Topolino. It stopped, and driving the car was the forest ranger. I heard my brother saying, "We are going to see our aunt in Caoria." Then the ranger continued his drive uphill. We waited until the car noise could no longer be heard before we returned to our tree. Then we took the tree and continued our walk home. We also had to collect moss for the base for the Crèche formation.

Now that I was bigger, I was allowed to help Pino set up the tree and Crèche. I liked being with Pino. He was always patient in explaining what had to be done. Then when I did something, I did it with more pleasure, more confidence. Real candles were placed on the tree, and they had to be placed so that the candle wouldn't burn the branch above. We had few glass balls. To make up for the shortfall of balls, we used biscuits as well. For the Crèche, we had a bigger selection of small figures of shepherds, sheep, and other animals. The three wise kings sat on camels and were placed farthest away from the Crèche stable. Then after Christmas day, they would be placed a bit closer every day until on the 6th of January when they would be by the stable.

Before school ended for Christmas, the teacher had asked me if I could have a haircut in preparation for a play she was preparing. At midday break, I went to the barbershop to have my haircut. Then some strange man came to the shop and said, "You are the grandson of Ignaz Risser, are you not?" "Yes," I replied. "Could you please do me a favor and take a message to your grandfather?" I hesitated because of my haircut. There was still a queue in front of me. If I left now, I wouldn't have got back on time to have my haircut. To go to my grandfather's place from there, even by running, would have taken about forty minutes. In the end, he offered me 100 lire. I gave in and took the message to my grandfather. The teacher didn't say anything; she simply looked at me with disappointment. There were two sisters that taught in this school, and they came from Egna, the next village to Laghetti.

Ignaz had come home for Christmas. My father was also present in the background. He didn't participate much in the joy we children felt for this festive period. He was around but left us kids to enjoy ourselves. It was baby Jesus who brought the presents. I received school items and biscuits and was excited to show my brothers what I had received, and my brothers closest to me were doing the same. They were just as excited as I was about the presents they had received.

During these festive days, all in the village were friendlier than the rest of the year. As usual, my mother would take one boy to the early mass while the others would go to the big mass. The church was so bitterly cold, but I felt the warmth of the people who crowded the church. Men used the right hand side stools in the church and at the rear. The stools at the front were for the children. Boys on the right, and girls and ladies on the left. The only problem was the cold. What made it even worse was that, on this day, the priest would hold the long service. It was so long that, for me, it was simply never-ending while my feet froze more and more. At times during the mass, I would look up at the window with my grandfather's name on it and feel proud to have been his grandchild. He was also seen as a wise man in the village. He had the best wine in the village, and that was confirmed by the men of the village.

One day, Ignaz got taken to the Magre train station with no explanation to me. I got left with the thought that he wouldn't be going "Ai Freschi" in the winter. But I soon realized that he had gone. When I would see him again was my question. I simply couldn't understand why nothing was said to the remaining brothers, that one of us would be going away and where he would be going and for how long. Lodovico wasn't to be seen either. Mario and Pino nearly always came home in the evenings. Occasionally, I even saw my father.

The water pipes, when installed, were laid part of the way on the surface of the ground. The overall length of the water pipe run was a few hundred meters; to dig the ground for that length would have taken a long time. In the summer, that was no problem, but in the winter, the water used to freeze in the pipes. To thaw out the water, I had to get straw, lay it around the pipes, and set it alight. Then

I had to lay more and more straw on the fire until the water started to run again. After this experience, the pipes got covered with straw, and the water was left running slightly at all times during the cold winter months. There weren't any water meters at that time.

My big brothers, who left every morning to get the train to go to work, needed a warm breakfast. It became my job to get up early, to light the fire in the stove and warm up the soup or whatever my mother had prepared for them in advance. Sometimes, the fire took a bit longer to get going, and the soup wasn't warm enough, and they didn't have the time to wait for it to get warmer. That meant that I got a telling off, and I had to get up a bit earlier in the mornings to make sure it didn't happen again.

At times, the kindling and firewood were probably a bit damp and didn't set alight that easily. The only fire lighter I had was paper. I made a habit of placing some wood in the oven while it was warm on the day before. That way, the wood was dry, and it set alight without hesitating the next morning, but that didn't mean that I could stay in bed longer. I couldn't run the risk of having cold soup for my brothers in the mornings before they went to work. After they left, I could have breakfast and had to prepare myself to go to church and school. Before my first communion, I used to like going to church, but I had lost some interest in it.

## CHAPTER TWELVE

SPRING STARTED IN APRIL, but in May, it came alive with an endless number of different green leaves and different color fruit blossoms. The cherry trees had finished their blossoming, but the apple, pear, almond, and peach trees were full of blossoms now. It was also cold enough so that the frost could damage the blossom. In the early morning, the fruit growing farmers went to the fields and lit fires. Therefore, they created a layer of smoke along the valley. The smoke cooled quickly and spread out just above the treetops. Looking down from my grandfather's farm, the smoke looked just like fog. The thing was, in this area, we didn't get fog. We got smoke to protect the blossoms. During this period, the priest would organize a procession, walking through the fields with the grass covered in dew. All this was held before the morning mass.

One day, Pino and I were just talking about all his experiences, and in return, I said something about my experiences too. He worked in Bolzano, and at times, he made it sound as if it was something, some town from a different world.

He told me that he had, for the first time, bought a yellow fruit called a banana. I had never heard the name banana before then. "So, what is it like? Was it good?" I asked. Well, he did take a long time to explain to me what a banana looked like and what it tasted like. He also told me about some experiences he had when he was a cow boy. He and Lodovoco had done the same thing as I had done during the last summer. I never asked, but I had the feeling that Mario went to the Musolini youth camps instead of going to work on the farms. Pino said that he had to take the herds to the pastures for several farmers. He went along the village and got a few cows from one farm and a few more from another farm. This he did until he had his complete herd. He took them up in the forest and looked after them all day. He was given bread for his morning break and corn flour for his lunch, which he had to cook with his utensils. In addition, he was given some cheese or sausage.

He would boil-cook the corn flour into polenta. That was like a pudding in a lump. It depended on how soft or hard it was made, the final shape it would have. This was a common food in this area of Italy and often eaten with goulash or sauerkraut with smoked pork boiled in the sauerkraut. Water was normally used to make polenta. Pino said, "At times, I milked a cow and used the milk to make my polenta." His milk-made polenta with cheese or sausage sounded like something good. He would also have his afternoon break before guiding the herd back to the village and to the individual farmers.

I told Pino about that new threshing machine the farmer had bought for threshing. I told him how much dust it made. Then, he spent ages telling me how to breathe in such cases. "Always breathe through your nose when there is dust where you are. If you do that, the hair in the nose will serve as a filter." Apart from the gas masks, we didn't know of any others masks.

In those days, to preserve food, they used different methods for different foods. To preserve cabbage, for instance, it was cut into thin slices then placed in a barrel with a lid that slid down inside the barrel. The cabbage was placed in layers in the barrel, and seasonings were added to each layer of cabbage. When the barrel was full, the lid was placed on top of the cabbage with some weights on the lid. The lid slowly sank, and after some days, it was covered by fluid from the cabbage. After a few months, it could be eaten as sauerkraut.

Milk was turned into cheese or butter to preserve it. Meat was salted or smoked for its preservation. Eggs were placed in a container with a chalky liquid and used during the winter when the chickens didn't lay eggs.

For some days, my mother wasn't at home, and my grandmother came to help out. My grandmother found a piece of meat, which was no longer of any use, in the larder. My mother had the bad habit of preserving food until it had gone bad. She saved it for a special occasion, and that occasion was when my grandmother threw it away with a grumbling mutter, "What is the point of saving it until it goes bad?" Meat was extremely rare in those days, and having to throw it away hurt my grandmother. It made me angry to see that her own sons weren't special enough to receive some cooked meat which she already had.

## CHAPTER THIRTEEN

SIUSI WAS A VILLAGE NORTH OF BOLZANO, and this was the new place where I would be staying. Toward the end of May, my mother once more took me to "Ai Freschi." This time, she came alone to take me to my destiny. We went to the station like last year. Only this time, we didn't get off at Bronzol. I simply didn't know where she was taking me. The train took us a lot further than Bronzol. We went past Bolzano and ended up in Castelrotto. This train stop had a small station in this narrow valley, which had road, river, and railway line nearly touching one another. It also had a stationmaster who blew a whistle after we had got off the train.

Just by the station, there was a wooden bridge, which we crossed. After the bridge, we started an uphill walk similar to last year. This time, we got to a farmhouse without first going through villages. At this farm, there was a lady who showed me to my bedroom just like last year. This time, I had a roommate, Peter. He was my age, and I wouldn't be as lonely as the previous year. This place was totally different from the other place. Getting up in the mornings was still at five, and milking was the same. The cows were guided to a field which was fenced in, with a three-rail pole fence. The gate was closed, and the cows were left to themselves.

Here, they were still threshing corn from the previous year. Next to this threshing machine, they had a wagon with high side constructed like a three-rail pole fence. Only this was more like a five-post fence. Two adults were throwing straw into this enclosure of the cart. The two boys had to trample the straw to squash it. The dust caused by the work was just incredible. I remembered what Pino said about dust. "Close your mouth, and breathe with your nose." We had to do this work all morning with a break at halfway.

Then came lunch. My nose was full of dust. I had to go to the fountain with running water to wash the dust out. At lunch, they served dumplings with salad. There was a tempting and gorgeous-looking meat salad. No one touched it during the meal.

Therefore, I didn't either. After we all finished eating dumplings and salad, the grownups started eating this meat salad. Peter didn't take any, and I was too embarrassed to take some, as Peter had been at this place longer than I had. I asked him after lunch why he didn't take any of the meat salad. He replied that it was only for the family and not for us. I felt that they should have eaten it in private. What they were doing was to torment us boys.

In the afternoon, we continued with the dusty job from the morning. As this job didn't get finished on this day, we had to continue on the next day. When this job was finished, we took off our shirts, and each one shook it to get the dust off it. The shirts were changed only once a week. When the washing was done by hand, there wasn't time to wash the clothing every day. The cows were guided to the stable only in the evenings for milking. Peter was, at times, a bit hateful to me. I never understood why he behaved like that.

After two weeks, I was asked to pack my things, and I was taken to another farm. The new farm was in Sant'Osvaldo St., close to Siusi. It was about twenty minutes to walk to the village of Siusi. Here, too, I got shown to my room by the lady of the house. This time the room was in the loft. It had two beds in it. I got the bed closest to the balcony. The wooden door that gave access to the balcony wasn't that airtight, and there was no window. Looking out from this door, I had the full view of the Siliar mountain in front of me. It seemed that it was there high up to look down on me.

*(This is the mountain I saw from my bedroom opening that led to the balcony.)*

I got left there to start a new event, a new experience. The people living here were the grandparents, their son, Luis, and his wife, Anna. They had one son, Paul, of about two years. All grown-ups were of medium build and looked fit. They all lived on the same floor, as the ground was on a slope. The road was about halfway between the floor with the living quarters and the loft. Then, as the ground sloped even further down, one could walk straight into the cellar without having steps. Walking down from the road to the house, one got faced by the loo door. There was the entrance to the house on the left of the loo door. Bedrooms, the kitchen, and dining area— plus there was the lounge with a bread-making oven.

The door to load the wood in the oven was in the kitchen. The oven was big and rounded at the top. It also had a flat wooden surface on top of the oven, where the farmer, on occasions, on Sundays, had a snooze. There was the farmyard separating the house from the barn and stables. At the end of the yard was the manure deposit. By raising one's eyes, one had a breathtaking view of the mountains. On my first day at this place, I was invited to eat and nothing else. They prayed before and after eating. Only after the evening meal, they sat at the table and prayed the whole rosary. After this, I was allowed to go to bed or do my own thing with limitations.

The mattress was like a sack the size of the bed. It was filled with maize leaves. When I was awakened at five, I left the shape of my body in the mattress. The imprint of my body in the mattress could clearly be seen. I was taken to the stable and shown what I had to do. First of all, I had to feed the animals. The farmer had male and female cattle of different ages. He had two pigs and chickens. Well, the cats were on all farms, so that goes without saying that there were cats. In the stable, I had to place some food in the mangers for the cattle, but before that, I had to clean the mangers. With a brush, I swept out the remains from the last feeding. After this, I had to clean the stable. I had to place all cow droppings in a wheelbarrow, take it outside, and empty the wheelbarrow on the manure heap. Then, I had to place new bedding on the floor for the animals.

After this, I had to groom the cattle. I was given a curry comb and a body brush. Curry comb in my left hand, and body brush in my right hand. I was shown to comb and brush in the same direction of the fur. When the farmer, Luis, and his father finished milking, the animals were let out to drink from the fountain. After this, it was seven in the morning, and we went to the kitchen to have breakfast, which was cooked by the farmer's mother. When I arrived at this farm, I wasn't introduced to the family. I just picked up the names as time passed and got to know that the farmer's name was Luis.

The breakfast was something special. It was mosa, a dumpling cooked in a big shallow pan and covered by pouring on it melted butter or elderberry sauce. It got placed on the table, and all ate direct from the pan. On the base of the pan, a crust had formed from the cooking. This got scraped by each person for the area that he had been eating from. This breakfast was adorable for me. After breakfast, we would go in the fields. Here, they didn't have any grazing pastures. They had fields with grass that was hand-cut with a sickle, raked together, and taken to the barn for the animals. The fields on this farm were all on slopes. To both sides of the farm buildings, the ground sloped gently, and the further away the ground went from the buildings, the steeper became the slopes. To both sides of the farm buildings, there were some retaining walls that had been built in the past, and the back of the walls had been filled with soil to obtain a more level ground.

Here, everything had to be carried by hand. The mowed grass was laid on a big cloth that looked similar to a double-bed sheet and had some knotting facilities on each corner. So, when there was enough grass on the cloth, the corners were tied together, and this big parcel was lifted onto the farmer's shoulder. He would then carry it to the barn. From the hay barn, there was a chute down to the stable. It became my job to throw down enough grass for the next feeding of the animals.

Then there was the weeding of the big acres to be done. The grain fields were not weeded, but the other fields had to be done. Potatoes, cabbages, beetroot, pumpkins, courgettes, etc. With a hoe, I had to hoe out the weeds from the rest of the plants. At times, Luis and I would do it together, and at times, Anna helped as well. This was a sort of soul-destroying job that never finish. I didn't have to do it in the vegetable garden, but in the big fields, when I finished the last row of the last field, it had to be started all over again.

On Sunday, after the stable tasks were done, and we had breakfast, they all dressed up. Anna would spend some time preparing Luis' hat with decorations. She would fix some background to the hat first and would end up with a red carnation. Here, they spoke in a German dialect and wore a typical Tirolean costume on Sundays. I walked with the farmers to church, which took about twenty minutes. The church was full of people, and most of them were dressed up in their local costume. Here, too, the men and boys were on the right of the church, and the ladies and girls on the left. Everyone was a stranger to me except my Luis, his parents, and Anna. Like always, the mass was held in Latin, and the sermon was held in German.

After the service, we all left the church, and outside, my brother Ignaz waited for me. He had seen me inside the church and made a point of speaking to me outside. Luis left me with Ignaz and told me not to be late for lunch. It simply didn't dawn on me that Ignaz would have been there too. He told me on which farm he was working. Actually, it was the closest farm to where I was. There was no road linking the two farms, but walking down the forest to the flat of the valley was only a few minutes. We both had Sunday afternoon free, but we had to be at the farm for the evening care of the animals.

Here, I received one more surprise. My cousin, Anna, was helping to run the house on the same farm where Ignaz worked. This cousin's home was in Egna, which was the next village to Laghetti, and I hadn't seen her that often. But I was looking forward to seeing her too. After lunch, I walked out the door to go down the forest to see Ignaz and Anna. My farmer stopped me and asked, "Where are you going?" "To my brother," I said. "I'll be back on time to do the stable." "Oh no," he said. "You can't disturb others whenever you like." It was my only afternoon off in the week, and I wasn't allowed to go to see my own brother.

One day, I was awakened in the early morning. In fact, it was much, much earlier than five. I was taken to the stable, and there we took four young animals of mixed sexes and started walking towards the village. I didn't have the slightest idea where we were going. We walked behind the animals and guided them past the village and up a hill in front of us. We walked and walked until we got to the top of this hill.

We had got to the Alpi di Siusi. "Siusi Alps." We had a break and had something to eat and drink. Luis had only taken wine in the rucksack, which I didn't like that much. After the break, we started walking and walking to the other end of the Alps. On the way, the farmer gave a break to the animals just for a few minutes. They simply grazed this gorgeous grass for a short time, and then we continued. At the base of the Sasso Lungo, there was an enormous pasture where we took the animals. There were many farmers who took their animals to this place and left them there for the summer.

At this place, Luis handed the animals to someone in charge, who, in turn, let them into a gate. Here, we had another break. The farmer offered me another drink of wine, which I refused, and I found some water. While we were eating, other farmers continued to arrive with their animals. So, the animals that weren't needed at the farm during the summer were brought here. The cows had to be milked; therefore, they had to be kept at the farm.

The time had come to begin the return walk. At one point, I got so thirsty that I drank some water from a dirty puddle formed by a cow's foot. It started getting dark, and we were still a long way from the farm. It got to a point that I started to fall asleep while I was walking. I was desperately fighting to keep my eyes open. We got home around midnight. We left at three and returned at midnight. We had been gone for twenty-one hours, and the vast majority of that time was used walking. The next morning, I noticed that the stable wasn't cleaned the day before when I was gone. I supposed that the important part was to milk and feed the cows, and the cleaning was left for me to do.

During the summer, I was allowed three times to see my brother and cousin. I was allowed to go to the village if there was a special event. On one occasion, there was a village event when everyone was dressed in costume. Men had long whips with short handles. There were several men standing some distance from one another and were using the whips to make loud BANGS in a rhythm. Fireworks weren't known in those days in this village or any other village where I had been. This was the biggest event of the year in this village. Apart from the whip tune, there were activities like pole climbing and dancing. The Schuhplattler dance was quite fascinating to watch. Only men participated in this dance. They had a local costume of leather shorts and leather braces, white socks to just below the knee, and white shirts. Part of the dance was two men holding themselves in opposite directions. One was standing normally, while the other was held or held himself with his feet upwards, and with their hands, they slapped each other's bottom. They would turn and change position, and the one standing on the ground before would now have his legs in the air, and the other one would be standing on the ground. It was interesting to watch if one hasn't seen it before.

This summer was extremely dry. The priest arranged a procession through the fields to pray for rain. I don't know if it helped. In desperation, one tries anything. A shortage of grass means a shortage of hay for the winter.

## Chapter Fourteen

A NEW EVENT OCCURRED. One morning, we left with one cow and walked to the Alpi di Siusi again.

*(This is part of the Alpi di Siusi in full blossom)*

This time, we ended up at a mountain hut. The hut was on top of a slight hill with fantastic panoramic views all round. This time, there were Luis, his mother, and me. Here, Luis cut the grass for the cow just like he did at home. In this area, it was all open. It was vast, and there was not a fence to be seen in any direction. The cow gave about three-quarters of a bucket of milk on the first milking. Then, the milk she produced increased, and the cream in the milk, at the least, tripled in volume. I asked the farmer why that was. He explained that the grass in this area grew very little, but in exchange, it was of extremely good quality.

My job was to get the water from a spring, which was three to four minutes away from the hut. It was a tiny spring on a gentle slope, which came out of the ground and was guided in a wooden channel a short distance to where it was high enough to place the bucket under the channel. The water came out so slowly that it took at least twenty minutes to fill a bucket.

I always walked barefoot in the summer. Here, there was a beautiful flower that must have belonged to the devil's family. It grew extremely close to the ground, with spiky leaves all around the plant, the flower in the center which sunk into the plant. Before the grass was cut, I could see them and avoid them. Once grass became hay, they were anywhere in the grass, and I constantly stepped on them. Their needles were so strong that once they penetrated the skin, they would stay stuck to the foot.

Luis prepared enough hay to use as a mattress for the help that was coming. After a few days, some young men and ladies came to help with the hay making. The men prepared their scythes for the next day. First, they all found a place where they could sit on the ground and fix a steel base in the ground. The top of this tool was especially made for the cutting edge of the scythe to rest on. Then, the cutting edge of the scythe was hit with a hammer to flatten the cutting edge.

Then, finally, it was sharpened with a hand-held sharpening stone. This stone was placed in a special holder with water and fixed to the waist of each man. When required, the scythe could be sharpened by each individual as needed. The ladies raked the cut grass into stripes several centimeters thick. When one side of the grass was dry, it would be turned to dry the other side. Here, when the dried grass had become hay, it was transported the same way it was at the farm. A big white cloth was filled with hay, then the opposite corners of the cloth were pulled tight and tied. This was now carried on the shoulder of a man to the hay barn, which was part of the hut. When we went to bed, each one of us took one hay carrying sheet, laid it on the hay, and then laid on the sheet. We would fold both sides over ourselves and pull sufficient hay on top to keep warm.

Here, when we got up in the mornings, no one washed. There were no washing facilities. One could have walked to the spring, but one couldn't strip to wash. The loo was a small hut added to the outside of the big hut and had a hole in the ground. Newspaper was cut into small squares and hung on a wire inside the loo. Often, the loo doors had a hole cut in the shape of a heart at eye level. I think that the heart-shaped hole was to let people see if the loo was occupied.

After a couple of weeks, we went from here to another hut. The other hut was in a dip and could not be seen until we got on top of it.

Around the hut, the ground was flat, and the grass was long. Around the edges of the flat area, the incline began. On about a third of the area, the slope up wasn't high, but on the rest, the incline was nearly endless. There was a water spring, which was just fantastic. It came directly from the ground, and in large quantities, it actually made a small stream.

The living habits here were identical to the other hut. The mother would prepare the food, while the others would make hay. The kitchen was a few meters square and had a built-up stone platform to cook on. A fire was lit in the center of the platform, where a steel tripod saucepan support was set over the fire. The legs of the tripod were outside the fire. One tripod leg was farthest from the fire and had a support for the handles of the saucepan to rest on. High up on the wall, there was a hole for the smoke to escape. There were shelves for the plates and kitchen utensils.

The stable was at the opposite end from the kitchen with the hay barn in the middle. On these fields, I hadn't seen one of the prickly leaves with the beautiful flowers. Once the hay making was finished, they all left except Maria and me. The cow was taken back to the farm, and the other non-milk-producing animals were brought to graze in this mountain pasture. I had to look after the animals while they were grazing. I had to keep them within the farmer's boundaries. The boundaries could be recognized by a strip of grass that wasn't cut during the hay making. The boundary line was also slightly raised. From the distance, a person wouldn't have seen them, but from nearby, they were obvious. They weren't so obvious to the cattle, and I had to be careful that they wouldn't cross the boundaries.

One day, I was looking in the direction of Siusi, which, from where I stood, was on the right of the impressive Siliar. I could see what seemed an enormous herd of sheep that had a slight reflection from the sun on their backs. I had never seen anything like it before. There were clouds below me. I had never seen the top of a cloud before. Now I could see how they came over the brow at the end of the Alps. They were moving quite fast, and in a short while, they were on top of me. Now I was surrounded in fog. It got thicker and thicker, and I was losing sight of the animals. I found them one by one and took them to the flat area by the hut. Surprisingly, they actually stayed there while I got the others one by one.

Then, on another occasion, the animals got nervous. They were flinging their tails around more than usual. Then unexpectedly, one animal would raise its tail above its body height and start to run. On one side of the hills enclosure where the hut was, there was an opening where the stream water could flow through. The animal used this opening to run through. It could have run in whichever direction, but it chose the lowest point. Then another heifer did the identical thing. I waited till the last one started to raise its tail.

I got hold of the tail, and when the heifer started running, it pulled me along too. I had never run that fast before. She took me to where all the others had run to. I got them all back to the correct pasture. Now the sky darkened, and the thunder from a storm was getting closer. I guided the animals into the stable to protect them from this storm that was passing over us. The lightning lit and shook the area in a scary way. Big drops started to fall, and I went indoors to Maria. I thought Maria, who looked after me, was old. She probably wasn't that old, and she just appeared old to me.

The lightning and thunder got constantly more intense. Then, there was a tremendous *bang* that shook the hut so much that the stored items on the shelves in the kitchen fell to the floor. After about half an hour, the rain slowly eased, and the thunder faded to the far. Now it was also getting dark; therefore, the animals were left in the stable. When I took the animals grazing in the fields the next morning, I made a point of looking around to see if that lightning had left any signs. In fact, on the brow of the hill, there was a new long channel in a zigzag form about twenty centimeters deep and approximately the same width.

On the other side of the brow of this hill, there was a steep drop of bare rock down to the fields some distance below. The animals, at times, grazed on the edge of this drop without hesitation, sure-footed. Instinct must have given them the feeling for how close to the edge they could go. Even on my field, some parts were so steep that the individuals of the herd would not walk there. At times, I sort of climbed up this slope, and to my surprise, one day, I found the first edelweiss that I had seen growing in nature. From hearsay, the edelweiss only grew on rocky surfaces and at a high altitude. Even the name Edel-weiss (equivalent to noble white) made it impressive for me. I sat there for a long time, admiring this joyful discovery.

*(The Edelweiss. The flower that lured so many young men into dangerous situations. Even Julie Andrews sang the famous song about this flower.)*

I occasionally glanced at the animals and would continue to gaze at this discovery. From now on, I would often look at its soft, furry petals, and I would look to see if there were any more beautiful wonders in the area. Oh yes! The big dark bluebells that were facing upwards. There was a vast variety of flowers on the Alps that only grew above a certain altitude. On occasions, I heard that some young man had an accident while trying to collect edelweiss from some rock face of a mountain and had fallen.

With the passing of time, I often went to look at the edelweiss I had found. Slowly, the petals started to become fluffy and lost their beauty. Yes, to find edelweiss and to be able to see on top of clouds, I must have been "Ai Freschi." The Siliar range was still higher, and I was longing to go up to it one day.

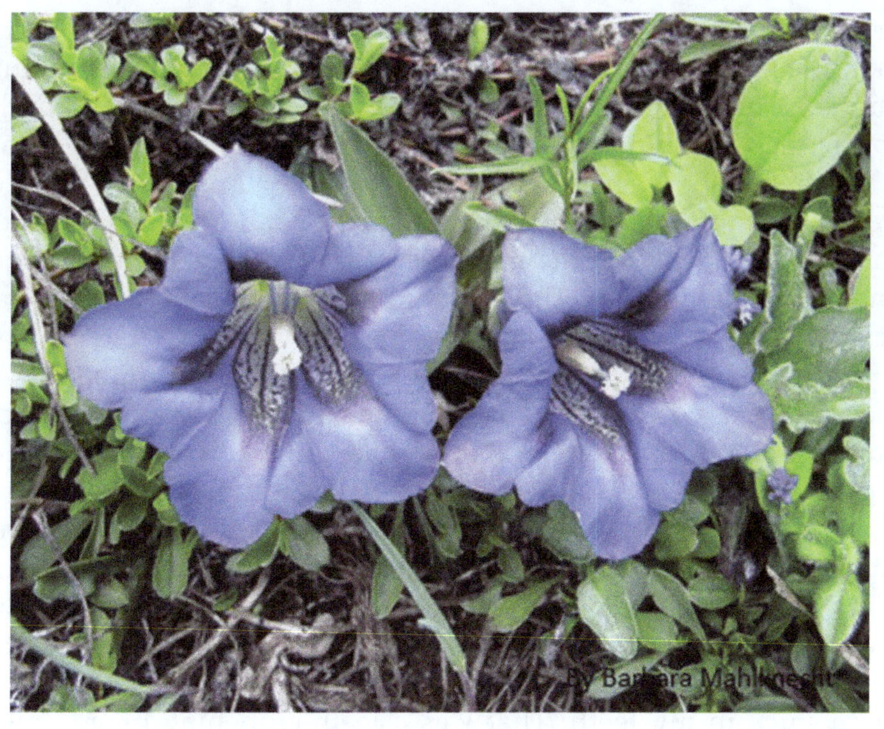

*(These are the natural vonders that grow on the alps.)*

Despite that, these people were religious. On Sundays, we didn't go to church while we stayed on the alps. Every day of the week was the same. Here, I couldn't hear the church bells or anything else that would indicate it was Sunday. Once the hay makers had gone, I wouldn't see another soul for weeks except for Maria. On occasions, Maria would send me to get some milk. That meant that I had to walk to the next nearest Alps resort that had a cow. I had to walk downhill for a long way to get the milk and then had to carry the milk uphill. Fortunately, I didn't have to carry much milk. I had to carry a two-litre aluminum urn with a lid. The farmers must have had some arrangement because I was never given any money for the milk.

Once, a stranger did come by. He was probably one of the

first foreign tourists in the area. Maria gave him some bread. He took the bread and went to the water spring. With an aluminum mug taken from his rucksack, he got some freezing water from the spring then found a place to sit and have a bread and water break. When he finished his feast, he came back to tell us, "I am a doctor from Germany, and what I just had was the healthiest meal a person could have. Then with the magnificent air you have here, it makes one's life like a dream. The air you have here is so fine that I can smell the Alps' scent in it."

I didn't even know what he meant with his comments. We didn't have any fresh bread at any time when we were on the Alps. Therefore, you can imagine that he had received hard bread. This farmer only had hard bread. This bread was extremely similar in shape and thickness to a normal Italian pizza without the topping. At the farm, it was stored in the loft in a special rack container. This pizza-like bread was placed in the rack in a vertical position, like plates in a kitchen rack. This bread was consumed on a daily basis and also taken to the Alps. It was so hard that, at times, I got a small piece stuck in my teeth. That was a teeth-crunching bread, but it did have a nice flavor. The whole pizza-like bread was held in both hands and broken into pieces. Then one took a piece for oneself and bit or broke some off to chew, and hopefully, the teeth didn't break.

On a daily basis, Maria and I didn't get on that well. She had her duties, and I had mine. I did what I had to do, but at times, she seemed to moan for no reason, and I argued back. One day, the farmer arrived, and he stayed for the night. The next morning, he took two oxen and fitted the cart to them. I had to go too. He took some wood-cutting tools, and we set off in the same direction we had gone with the animals on that early morning start when we didn't get home till midnight. We went to the forest in that area, and there, we collected firewood to be used at the hut. The trees had been felled, and we had to saw them into sections that would fit on the cart.

Luis had a big saw with a wooden handle on each side. He

pulled it from one side, and I did the same on the other side. That was physically hard work. Then carrying the sawn trunks to the cart was just killing me. The cart was left on the flat surface higher up outside the forest, and we had to carry these extremely heavy tree trunks up the slope to the cart. I just couldn't believe what hard work I had to do to earn my daily bread, which, by the way, broke my teeth. After the cart was loaded, the load was tied firmly to the cart, and we returned to the hat. When horses pulled a cart or a wagon, we sat on the load pulled by them. With oxen, we had to be at the front of them to guide them. That was normally my job, while the farmer walked alongside the cart. By the time we got back, it was quite late. The oxen were taken from the cart and led to the stream to have a drink. Then in the stable, they were given some hay. After this, we went in the kitchen and had some food too.

The unloading was done the next day. Now all the tree trunks were placed one by one on a frame and were sawn into logs to be used for firewood. Then the farmer showed me how to split them into firewood, and where I had to pile them once they were chopped. Once all the trunks were sawn to logs, the farmer returned home. It took me weeks of my spare time to split all the logs. I still had to take care of the animals. Some logs were thick and heavy for me to handle. One big log was prepared to be used as a base log. Then just like the farmer showed me, I placed a log on top of the big log. Then with the cutting edge of the axe, I would hit the log as hard as I could. That move was only good enough to fix the axe into the log. Then I had to lift the axe with the log attached to it, turn the axe round to make the head of the axe hit the chopping log. This way, the weight of the log would press on the cutting edge of the axe and hopefully split. If it didn't split the first time, I had to repeat that move until it did split. This gave me two halves of the log. Then I had to repeat the same procedure with each half, just like I did with the whole log. Only after the big log was split into two did it become much easier to split a half of the original log. I had to let the cattle out each day and keep an eye on them from where I was chopping the logs. If one of them went astray, I had to go and get it back. The roof of the hut had an overhang big enough to protect the chopped firewood from the rain and snow.

## Chapter Fifteen

ON ONE OCCASION, MY MOTHER, Lodovico, and my cousin, Franz, had come to see me, but they wanted to continue and walk up to the top of the Siliar. I was longing to go with them, and Maria let me go. From the hut, on rare occasions, I could see a person or a few people walking on a path up the side of the mountain. The path was in a serpentine shape and was narrow. I wondered what and how far could they see from the top of the Siliar. Now the time had come that I could see for myself. In comparison to the Alps, it was really cold on top of that mountain. Up there, it was high enough to see the mountain peaks in Switzerland and Austria. That was what the grown-ups said. Ah yes, that peak is "whatever it was," and that was in Switzerland or Austria.

Photo by Barbara Mahlknecht

From the distance, a winding path can be seen going to the top of the mountain. There was a bar-restaurant up there too, and we were the only people there. We had eaten outside but went to the bar to have a drink. I received an orange drink. The waiter came with the bottle and opened it at the table. Then, he poured the fizzy orange into a glass, and I started sipping it as if it had to last forever. This was the first time that I had received a fizzy drink. By the time we got back, it was dark, and they all slept in the beautiful hay aroma.

From the Alps, we returned to the farm in time for harvesting. We returned with the animals without any fuss. But there were the bigger farmers that would return from the Alps in great style. They decorated the cows' heads with elaborations of flowers and green branches. They would also have enormous bells hanging on a strap fastened around their neck. The bells were all of different tunes, and they could be heard from a long way off. Most farmers had a wagon with crostoli covered in powder sugar to attract the children.

*(Photo of the area)*

The heads of the cows of the bigger farmers were decorated for the return trip from the alps to the villages. Back at the farm, all that had been planted would now be ripe and had to be harvested. The grain was cut by hand, and for this purpose, some extra help was present. The ladies would cut the plants with a sickle and place them in a small heap. The farmer would then tie them into a bundle, and a hired man would carry them to the hay barn. The fields were too steep to use a cart in most parts of this farm. At ten, Maria came with a snack and drinks. Well, that was the best snack I had in a long time: boiled potatoes, cut in halves, still with the peel on them. The flavor of those potatoes was simply delicious. Then, there was cheese and thinly sliced delightful speck. This was a feast and not just a simple break. All the bundles of grain that had been carried to the hay barn were piled up to one side of the hay floor. After the grain harvest ended, the hired labor left, and we did the rest of the harvesting by ourselves.

*(Cows returning home at the end of the summer with big bells and decorations on their heads)*

I disliked the potatoes harvest most of all. After the stable work, which started at five, we had breakfast and then went to the potato field with oxen and a special tool that went under the potatoes and raised them to the surface as it was being pulled by the oxen. I had to guide the oxen, and Luis would hold and guide the tool. After the whole field had been finished with this job, we started to pick up the potatoes. Anna helped as well. Each one of us filled our bucket and took it to a wheelbarrow. From this field, we could wheelbarrow them to the cellar. In the mornings, it was cold. It was so cold that after a while of picking up potatoes, my hands froze to the point that I couldn't grab a potato with my fingers. I had to use both hands to pick up one potato.

Luis showed me how to warm my hands without a fire. He flung his arms round his own body until he had them warm. Well, if it functioned for him, then I had to try it too. It actually functioned. The only problem was that I got a sort of pins and needles feeling in my fingers. That passed after a bit, and my hands became warm again. After all the harvesting was done, we started on other jobs.

By now, the autumn had demonstrated its beautiful colors and had made the leaves and needles drop from the trees. It was only the larch trees that lost needles in the autumn. All other pine trees kept a faithful green all through the winter. At this altitude, the autumn colors weren't as spectaculars as they were in the valleys, which were at a lower altitude. In the valleys, there was a greater variety of fruit trees. In turn, they gave a spectacular display of colors in the spring and autumn. In the spring, the display of different greens was just endless in the valleys. In addition, there were the blossoms from different fruit trees and vines, which were like a blanket that covered the valley. In the Siusi region, there were few fruit trees. Plums seemed to be one of the rare fruits that grew at this height. Therefore, the color change from spring to winter wasn't as spectacular as it was in the valleys lower down.

Now that the leaves and needles had fallen, bedding for the animals was collected for the winter and beyond. Apart from straw, they also used foliage, which had to be collected in the forest. My room companion, Naz, would help Luis rake up the leaves and fill a large basket, which I had to carry on my back. The straps were simple, flexible plant branches which were twisted like a plait. I had to walk up a steep hill to the forest and return loaded with bedding for the animals. In the mornings, as I was still walking up and down this hill, I could see the school children walk past on the street that led to the school. They had been doing it for some time, and I was wondering when I could go to school with them. Naz was, in fact, Luis' brother-in-law. We shared the room in the loft with our beds in it. In exchange for the rent, Naz would help with certain jobs when he had the time. He was an animal ranger for a large area and was seldom to be seen.

After a few weeks, they finished with the animal bedding and started on a new job. Now I had never seen this work being done before. In the acres that were ever so steep, the weather during the year washed some soil to the bottom of the field. Now the soil of about a meter-wide stripe of the lowest part of these fields was, in fact, taken to the top of the fields. For this job, they had a specially made three-wheel wheelbarrow with a strong steel ring on the front. A long rope was attached to the ring. The rope was passed behind the wheel of a pulley, which was firmly fixed at the top of the field and attached to oxen at the other side of the pulley. Basically, there was a wheel that was holding a rope from the top, with the oxen on one side and the three-wheel barrow on the other side. The wheelbarrow was loaded at the base of the field. When it was filled, the oxen walked diagonally down the field. As they walked down, the trolley came to the top of the field. Once it was at the top, it got emptied. I would undo the rope, and the person at the top would hold the rope to control the descent of the trolley to the bottom of the field. I would take the oxen back to the hoist and repeat the procedure all day, and for many, many, days.

One day came the time that I was allowed to go to school. At school, I was the novelty, and it seemed as if all children were around me. So many questions they had. After the first week, this curiosity effect started to ease, and by the end of the second week, there wasn't one person that spoke to me. On the third week, they started to see me as something to be attacked— verbally and physically. This was the worst time of all. I was something that could be made to feel despised by all around him. Walking home one day, there was the usual group of children that walked this way on every school day. They were in front of me because I had to collect the aluminum milk can, which I had to take to a family on the way to school. This was a regular milk delivery I had to do on my way to school. On my returning home this day, all the children that walked my way and a lady with a walking stick, whom I didn't know, were standing, blocking my way. As I went to walk past them, they stopped me and started pushing and insulting me. The lady with the walking stick was waving her stick as if she wanted to hit me.

As I saw the stick coming in the direction of my head, I managed to grab it and take it from the lady. I held the stick horizontally, and with it, I pushed a few children and the lady towards the three-board fence on the side of the road. The fence gave way, and they all fell backwards down the hill on the road side. The most spiteful boy was one of those who fell. I didn't stop to see what the result was of the falling; I just ran home to the farm. Ages after that incident, they came past the farm on their way home. From now on, their behavior became normal, just as if nothing had happened. I made a few friends like all do, and the others treated me as one of the class. The same thing had happened to Ignaz. He actually sent the biggest boy in his class to the doctor. After that episode, they became friends.

I was given homework to do like all the others in the class. The problem was that I couldn't start doing my homework before eleven at night. More than once, the farmer woke me from sleeping at the kitchen table with my homework under me. Normally, I did try to go to sleep at midnight. I had to get up regularly at five; therefore , I couldn't go to bed much later than midnight. Then, on occasions and unexpectedly, Luis would say, "Today, you are not going to school." That meant that I would have lost another day from school. I lost weeks of schooling at the beginning of the school year, and now he was keeping me at home to work. I was nearly crying from the disappointment.

In the hay barn on the floor, there was a special area with a harder wood flooring than the rest. Since I had been there, I had noticed that one area of flooring was different, and I didn't know why. Now the bundles of grain were laid on this floor in two rows and with the grain part in the middle with a space in between the two rows. Now four men would hammer the center of the double row with special tools. The tool had a long handle, and at the end, it had a round wooden club tied with a leather strap. The four men started the threshing by hammering these clubs on the grain heads. Two men were walking backwards, and two forwards with the heads of the clubs in the center of the four men. In a rhythm, they hammered at the straw heads. They started at one end and worked their way, threshing away to the other end.

It was my job to turn the straw bundles that had been threshed upside down. Therefore, as soon as the men finished in one direction, I would turn the bundles to the end, and then they would start in reverse. At the end of the second threshing, the straw got separated as much as possible from the grain. The grain was then piled to one side and the straw to another side. This job took more than one week to do. Then there came the job of purifying the grain from other particles. By turning a handle, a machine created a draft where the grain fell. The air pressure separated the small straw particles from the grain, and you can't imagine how much dust it made. To think that the machine used by the farmer I worked for last year would have done the threshing and cleaning the corn in one day.

For lunch, Maria nearly always made dumplings with white flour. I simply loved them and had five or even six. Being a Christian family, on Fridays, they made dumplings with dark flour and no meat, and they were horrible. They were so horribly dry that it took me the whole lunchtime to eat one. On rare occasions on a Friday, spaghetti was made with plum jam instead of the dark dumplings. That was jam they made themselves. No other jam would be bought. Spaghetti with jam was like a treat for me, and from my point of view, they could have made that every Friday.

Luis would take a load of grain, which had been placed in sacks, to the mill. Then about one week later, he came home with a big load of bread. There was so much freshly baked bread on that load that it would last for a whole year. At the beginning, it was absolutely gorgeous. Then it started to get rubbery, until, at the end of the second week, it was hard. Now for the next eleven month and two weeks, we would have hard bread. To obtain bread crumbs, Maria used a wood plane and planed the side of the bread, which got smaller and smaller. She had the plane in one hand and the bread in the other, and she simply planed the bread along the edge and got crumbs from it.

For the evening meal, a sort of soup was prepared. It was made of flour mixed with little water or milk. Stirring this mix turned it into small pellets, which were cooked in milk. On most occasions, that was the evening meal. Then, after the evening meal, they held the prayer time for an hour or thereabouts. It felt to me as if it would never end.

During the prayer, Anna would normally sit at the table and repair clothing. At other times, she would cut our hair. Only she would cut our hair, and no one else. The ladies in this family never got their hair cut. Nearly all ladies in the village had their hair made into a plait and then formed into a ball at the back of their head. Nothing was done for beauty except on Sundays. Even on Sundays, the hair would be the same as every other day. It was just the clothing that was elegant on Sundays for men, ladies, and for children too.

In the mornings, I had my daily chores to do before going to school. Here, the school children went to church before going to school, just like they did in Laghetti. I normally couldn't get to mass before school started. After I finished in the stable, I had breakfast, took the milk to a family in the village, and by the time I got to church, the others were about to come out. Once, I waited outside for the others to come out of church. After a few minutes' wait, they came out in procession and walked from the church to the school. I joined the end of the queue. The teacher had seen that I was waiting outside. I assume that it was for that reason that she, in the classroom, grabbed me by my hair and slapped my face, without giving a single explanation. When she let go of me, she had a handful of my hair. Now I could go to my desk. There were times that I was fighting to keep my eyes open during the school time. I seemed to get close on five hours of sleep, and that probably wasn't enough for a boy my age. As soon as there was a boring subject, my biggest problem was to stay awake.

## Chapter Sixteen

DURING THE WINTER, at times, it got overcast and mild. Mild was at about 0º, and that was when it normally started to snow. I absolutely loved to see the big snowflakes hovering to the ground in total silence. Then we had to clear the yard of snow before the animals walked on it. The cleared snow was placed beyond the yard and next to the manure heap. During the winter, this snow heap got quite high. Then in the spring, it was still melting when, in the fields, grass was growing.

Christmas was getting close, and I was allowed to go home for this special period. Yes, from Christmas Eve till the sixth of January, Ignaz and I were allowed to go home. We walked together to the small train station of Castelrotto. Yes, that was the same station where I had got off sometime in May. The train was a local train that stopped at every station. After some time, the train finally got to Magre, and we walked home. The tree and crèche had been prepared and were finished at my arrival.

Now, at last, we were all together for a bit. Three of us slept in a double bed. My mother slept in the kitchen, the bigger brothers in another room, and my father in his. Like clockwork, I woke up at five, just like I had gotten used to. I was awake and had nowhere to go. I wanted to get up, rather than lying awake in bed. In the end, I heard some movement in the kitchen, and I got up. It was seven in the morning. That meant that I was there in bed, doing nothing for two long hours. How boring. Then, at last, I could have a look to see what presents I had received. I most probably hadn't been good enough to have received some toys or something gorgeous to eat. Usually, I received supplies for school. It didn't take long before all the others got up as well.

Going to church, I felt as if I was the long, lost son who had returned. This was the first time that I didn't go to school in this village. All my old school companions and friends wanted to know why I wasn't coming to school. "Where are you now?"they would ask. "What are you doing? Are you staying now, or are you going away again?" Etc., etc. I felt quite chuffed in a way. One of the boys did insult me. To have seen the joy of all the others made up for that insult. To have seen my cousins and grandparents was simply great and so joyful.

After a while, I realized that I had to go home for my lunch. At home, we miraculously had a tranquil lunchtime. On this special occasion, we brothers stayed together as much as possible. There was a differing variation of having two age groups. Pino hovered between both. He could converse with the two oldest brothers and the three youngest as well. He hadn't changed from having received that belt slash down his back from my father. He was still good at telling the stories of films he had seen. This time, there was a corridor separating my father's room from our room. The walls were thick and made of stone and concrete. So, our father didn't get disturbed anymore during story telling.

In conversing, I was asked what I had received for my birthday. In fact, I had forgotten that I had a birthday this year. I didn't think that the farmer knew when my birthday was. In the new house, we still had the handmade light switches. During this period, my parents received little attention from us boys. My mother had a habit of becoming ill on such occasions. That way, her boys would all gather around her sofa bed for a while. Then, one by one, they all left her, and she was alone once more. On the next day, she would still be in bed and complain that she was being neglected. "No one brings me anything. For what you all care, I could just as well die," were her usual complaining remarks.

After about one week of me being at home, I got used to staying in bed till seven, and I didn't wake up at five in the mornings. The boring waiting time from five to seven had passed. On New Year's Day, it was just as exciting as it was on Christmas Day. I saw all the boys and girls I had seen on Christmas Day. Their curiosity hadn't diminished since the last time I had seen them.

Some boys told me that the farmer I had worked for the first year had come to Laghette get me for this year as well. Then I mentioned it to my mother, and she confirmed it. Then she added, "It is more convenient to have you both in the same village. This way, if I go to see one of you, I can see the other one as well." That was probably another reason why she took me to this different farm a long time before the school finished for the summer holiday.

Now I had also discovered that no one was informed about me having been moved from first farm to the one where I was now. It was just like taking a cow to the market. One would take her there, sell her, and no one would ask any questions. Well, when my mother came to see me, she did go to the first farm where I had been taken. Then, she discovered that I wasn't there any longer. My father had also come to see Ignaz and me during the summer. The only problem was that I was on the Alps and didn't see him. He had brought a rucksack with apples and gave half of them to Ignaz, and the other half he left for me at my farm. Strange that Luis didn't tell me, and also strange that I didn't receive a single apple of mine. In the cellar, Luis could have preserved some for me. The only present that my father had brought had been hidden from me.

The farmers where I had been the first year ended up finding another boy that was or had been in my class. Now I would say good bye to my friends, realizing that I wouldn't see them for another year.

On this occasion, I didn't have the time to slide down the ice slope. That had probably become a slide for the small boys. After the new year, the normal home routine commenced for my big brothers. Mario and Pino left in the mornings and would return in the evenings. Lodovico left, and I didn't see him again. Klaudio, Ignaz, and I were still there. On the sixth of January, Ignaz and I left to go back to our separate farms. After us leaving home, there would have been only Klaus left there, plus the two that returned every evening. Ignaz and I went alone to get to the train station. My father was never present to say "goodbye" to me. My parents were incapable of showing some or any form of love or affection for us children. I felt as if I was a constant inconvenience to my mother. Then, for my father, we hardly existed. There was no discrimination or favoritism shown between the boys. At least, that was the way it seemed to me. Then, when I got a bit bigger, I did notice that Pino was the favorite of my mother. We were all treated the same as each one of us went through that specific age. But now it was Ignaz's and my turn to be sent back to where we had come from: "Ai Freschi." Individually, Ignaz and I were taken just for the first time to where we would be staying, after which we had to go alone.

At the farm, it was the same as before Christmas. Nothing had changed. In the mornings, I felt the difficulty of getting up at 5 AM again. Then, after the first week of this early morning punishment, I got used to it and was awake before the farmer came to wake me. At the farm, there were still a lot of jobs to be done that could be done in the winter. One day, instead of going to school, I was told to empty the toilet pit. I was given two buckets, which I had to lower in the pit to fill them with that suffocating-smelling mixture of liquids and solids. Then I had to walk to the nearest field that was not plowed and empty the buckets. They had to be emptied evenly along the field; therefore, I had to walk further and further with each load I carried. How could human shit smell so horrible, and how could it be such a strong, suffocating smell? The cow manure that I piled in a big heap just outside the stable hardly had a smell. I was beginning to develop disrespect for Luis. First, he kept me home instead of letting me go to school, and in addition, he got me to do this hateful job, for which I should have had a gas mask. I was beginning to feel like the farm's slave. I don't know what Luis was doing during this time, but it certainly wasn't a hateful job like mine. It took me two days to empty that pit.

After this job, there was the job of taking the cow's manure to others fields and spread it there. I would be allowed to go to school for a few days, and then there was another job to be done and another. The hay had to be transported from the Alps to the farm.

I was taken along to trample the hay on the cart as it was being loaded. The fields had to be plowed, and I had to lead the oxen that pulled the plow. Luis controlled the plow. We walked from one end of the field to the opposite end. Then we would turn and come back in the opposite direction. The plow blade could be turned so that it would turn the soil in the same direction as before. Going one way, the soil was turned from right to the left, and on the return, it was turned from left to right. On these descending fields, the soil was always turned from the higher side to the lower side.

This was a slow job and kept me from school for many, many days. With all the fields that had to be plowed, it took weeks. They weren't done— one field after the other. He gave the oxen a rest in between, plowing one field and another. After the plowing, the oxen pulled a big square rake contraption over the plowed soil to make it flat and easy for sowing. After the sowing, the raking job was done once more to cover the seeds and hide them from the birds.

Easter was getting near, and at school, we had a mathematics test. The first to finish correctly would receive a chocolate Easter egg. The test we had to do was simple, and I was the first to finish it. I took it to the teacher, and she said that I had made a mistake. Then another boy finished it as well, and he got the prize. I checked and double checked my work and couldn't find the mistake. I returned to the teacher and said that I could not find the mistake. She then had another look and admitted she had made the same mistake as the other boy, but now the teacher couldn't take the chocolate egg from the false winner. He had already started to eat it. If it had not been the same teacher that pulled my hair and slapped my face, I would most probably have thought that she had made a mistake. But her being who she was, she must have done it deliberately. An honest teacher would have bought another chocolate egg for the true winner of the test. So, even here, the teacher discriminated against me for some unknown reason. I simply couldn't understand what I had done to her to make her behave like she did towards me. No other pupil got treated like me by this teacher.

Because there was such shortage of rain on the previous year, Luis got a bricklayer to build a big water container. Some way up the hill, there was a spring, but he needed to accumulate the water to obtain the volume and pressure for the sprinklers. The bricklayer needed help, and who ended up helping him? You guessed it. He wanted help with mixing the mortar and placing it just where he wanted it, getting stones for him, and placing them where he wanted them. All this work was done instead of me going to school. To get the materials from the street up to where the water tank was being built, they used the same three-wheeled cart used to move the soil from the bottom to the top of the fields.

For the work of pulling the materials to where they were needed, a man was hired with a motor contraption that pulled the cord that the cart was fixed to. The contraption had a cylinder fixed to it on which the cord wound around. Luis, Anna, and I loaded the cart. After the bricklayer was on his finishing stages, the plumber started to fit the pipes. The pipes going from the tank down to the fields were in light metal and had a quick coupling at one end. In dry weather, the water sprinkler was used, and it functioned like a dream. People walking by stopped to look at the sprinkler. Unfortunately, the tank was too weak to withhold the pressure of the water, and it formed a crack in the walls. The bricklayer did come to have a look. After seeing the split in the walls, he said, "I did say from the start that we should have used steel in the walls. For such a pressure, one must have steel-reinforced concrete walls and not just a normal stone wall." Nothing was done about the split in the walls, and the system couldn't be used.

Despite the shortage of rain, the water in the farmyard fountain was left running all the time. They simply made a bypass from a constant stream to the fountain. And if the water was constantly running in the fountain, it wouldn't freeze in the winter.

Apart from this job, which was an exception, firewood had to be collected from the forest and prepared like we had done on the Alps. Here, we collected the timber from the other side of the valley.

It was immediately under the Siliar mountain. To get there, we had to get to Siusi first and then along the valley on the opposite side to where the farm was. This time, the tree trunks, after they were sawn, were pulled downhill to the cart instead of uphill like we did on the Alps. Thank goodness for that, I thought. Whichever way, it was always hard work having to saw, move, and load those heavy tree trunks onto the cart. Once we got back to the farm, we had to unload them and then return to get more. Once we had transported all the tree trunks, they had to be sawn and split like I had to do on the Alps. The split tree trunks were stacked under the roof overhang from the hay barn. As the firewood storage was on the side of the street, once the timber was stacked under the roof overhang, it was marked with paint, hopefully, to stop the logs being stolen.

On rare occasions, I met up with Ignaz, and he told me the difference between his conditions at his farm and mine. He was given a bigger variety of foods, and he was seldom absent from school. He had a very good relationship with the people where he was. Plus, he had the pleasure of having a bit of company from our cousin, Anna.

From now on, the jobs of last year repeated themselves. I was more grown up, and I knew where we would go when we set off for somewhere, like the 3 AM start to take young animals to the very back of the Alps, a day when we would be walking for twenty-one hours minus the breaks. This year, I appreciated more the lush meadows with beautiful flowers and fresh herbs. The scenery was familiar too. Then, we got to the place where Luis, the previous year, had let his animals graze for a few minutes. There, the proprietor of that meadow was waiting for us, and he had a stern discussion with Luis about letting his cattle graze the year before.

From somewhere, he had watched with binoculars to see if anyone would let his cattle graze on his field while walking the animals to their summer retreat. It can be understood. If it were just one farmer with a few cows that grazed for a few minutes, it wouldn't be noticed. But today, it would have been busy with farmers who had come from far away, bringing their cattle through this field. If everyone stopped to graze, by the end of the day, there wouldn't be any grass left for his animals.

*(Cows grazing)*

At the farm, Luis' son, Paul, had become a brother. But Paul himself was about three by now. He was a nice, gentle boy and had his own little whip to play with. He chased chickens with it, and at times, he would also use it on the cows, and once he used it on me. I grabbed the whip from him and threw it as far as I could. Then he started to cry. Luis heard him and came to see what was happening. I explained what had happened, and the story finished there. Paul never did it again. But his mother had a nasty habit of pricking me in the arm. After the evening meal, she did her clothes mending while we prayed for an hour or so. At times, I did fall asleep during this boring hour. Then she would wake me by pricking me with a needle in the arm. One day, I got angry at her and told her to stop doing it. She didn't do it again.

At school, I was settling in and was making close friends. Anneliese was always nice to me, and she became my favorite in the class. She had shoulder-length hair and was always nicely dressed. She often wore a multi-pleated skirt, which opened delicately like a bell. She often had a gentle smile that would make me feel that she liked me. At times, in the winter, she would show me how many jumpers she had on and say, "Aren't you cold with just a shirt and jacket?" We spoke during the school breaks but never met outside the school.

When the temperature dropped close to 0º, that was nearly always an indication that it would snow. If the temperature rose from -15 or even -20º to 0º, the 0º temperature felt like a warm spell. Then it would most probably snow and snow. At times, it snowed with big flakes that nearly covered my hand. When it snowed, the silence was simply incredible. Even the animals had nothing to complain about on these occasions. Then, when the sky cleared, the scenery in all directions changed to a clean, fresh white. The tired-looking green trees in the forest suddenly became reborn with a fresh white. The temperature would drop to what it was before it snowed, and the sun would make the frozen snow glitter.

The priest was searching for singers and went in the classes and asked each student to sing a short part. Then he formed a choir for the church. That church was so incredibly cold in the winter; my freezing feet made my nearly cry. Generally, I got used to the cold. My bedroom was as cold as the outside. There was no heating, and the gaps round the door would let the cold enter as if the door hadn't been there. When I went to bed, it took ages before I was warm enough to go to sleep. Then once I was warm, I slept well.

My roommate Naz was rarely present. He was a ranger and wasn't working in this area. He worked occasionally at the farm when an extra hand was needed. He had two double-bore rifles, and he always left one in our room. He left a spare set of binoculars too. Those binoculars were so powerful that when I looked though them at the Siliar, I had the feeling that I could touch it.

## Chapter Seventeen

COMING INTO THE SUMMER THIS YEAR, I was also allowed to take the end of school exams. Since 1950, I was taken from school long before the exams took place. On the school report of this year, I had seventy-seven unjustified days of absenteeism. Not one of those missing days from school was because of illness. During one school year, there are approximately 165 school days. From 365 days in a year, we detract the three-month summer holidays, plus two weeks for Christmas, one week for Easter, plus Saturday and Sunday for the weeks that are left, leaving 165 school days. This meant that I failed to go to school 46 percent of the time without any official intervention. The system knew of this and did nothing to prevent it. Just think how much I had to work to earn my living. From five in the morning till eight in the evening. Those are fifteen hours. Less half an hour for breakfast, one hour for lunch, and two fifteen minutes for the morning and afternoon breaks. That makes it thirteen hours a day and six days a week. Then, on Sundays, it would have been two hours in the morning and two in the evening. That makes it eighty-two hours a week. Then, on the days I went to school, it would have been four and a half hours a day and a full day on Saturday plus Sunday. That was thirty-nine and a half hours a week. For Luis, that wasn't enough, and he kept me from going to school as well.

I was really beginning to feel ashamed for my bad reading. It got to the point that I hated to read aloud in class. Dyslexia wasn't recognized as some sort of illness in those days. I was classified as stupid by the other children and probably the teachers as well. To overcome this problem of mine, this new teacher, too, gave me reading aloud as homework. How could I read aloud in someone else's house? Plus, I didn't really understand what I was reading, and reading got tremendously boring for me. It took me probably half an hour to understand one page of a book. After that, the book would be placed to one side and dusted occasionally.

I found it strange that I could be top of the class in mathematics and bottom of the class in reading. During the day, I would practice the sums table until I knew it by heart. At times, I realized that it was easier for me to think 5 X 6 rather than 6 X 5. Often, if the reply to a mathematical question didn't come immediately, I would reverse the numbers. To calculate 9 X 7 was easier than calculating 7 X 9. To take 7 of 70 was easier than it was to take 3 X 9 of 90. Obviously, once I knew all the tables by heart, it didn't make much difference. So, I couldn't understand why some at school weren't good at math in the same way as they didn't understand why I wasn't good at reading.

The time had come that we would have gone to the Alps again for the summer. Everything was just like the previous year. First, we went to the hut on the brow of the hill. While we were hay making here, my mother came and helped for a few days, and she brought some old relatives from Innsbruck. They were thinking of staying for one week. But after one night's sleep in the hay, they had enough and left on the next day. Sleeping in the aromatic hay was quite an event. The hay had a glorious scent. It had an indescribable scent of mountain flowers that turned my thoughts into dreams. The grown-ups said how good it was to breathe that air. As to the breathing point of view, to me, it didn't make any difference. I simply loved the aroma and being surrounded by hay. So much so that only my face was left uncovered. My mother did stay a few more days and helped to rake the cut grass.

After the hay making was finished, there were just Maria and me left, just like last year. This year, the two of us got on well together. After she got to know my mother, she appreciated that I was somebody's son and not just a thing. After this, she was nicer to me than the year before. On the Alps, I lost the sense of the days of the week, just like the year before. There was just nothing to differentiate one day from the others. I simply didn't know if it was Monday or Saturday. What did it matter? We didn't go to mass on Sundays, and that would have been the only guide we normally would have had.

On a sunny day, one could see the approximate time from shadows on specific rocks or where the sun was in the sky. That wasn't an exact time, but it was sufficient for our needs. Then the animals had a good sense of timing. Often, some animals would start to return to the stable by themselves and at the correct time. "So how did they know what the time was?" was my thought. It must have been the same inbuilt timing, like waking up at five.

My brother, Mario, had come to see me in his military uniform. I did feel proud to have a brother in uniform, and I was proud of him even if he had not come in uniform.

After we left the Alps and returned to the farm, life returned to the usual routine. Before I left for the Alps, there was a thunderstorm, and the heavy hailstones smashed some branches of the flowers. I took one of the broken branches and placed it in a jar of water and placed it on an external cellar windowsill. I had totally forgotten about that broken branch that I had placed in water. Then when I returned from the Alps, that branch had become a lot bigger, which really pleased me.

There were some unexpected events as well. A brother of Luis bought a radio. Luis and Anna went to his brother specifically to listen to the novelty. Then there was a time that Luis couldn't walk. He had something malfunctioning with his knee for a week. During this time, Anna did the milking. During the morning hours in the stable, not a word was said between the person doing the milking and me. We got on with our jobs until we finished. After which, we went to have our breakfast. As soon as Luis got better, he returned to his duties.

My first job in the stable was to clean the continuous manger. I did that with a brush. To do this job quicker, I passed from one cow to the next by walking under the neck of the cows. This way, I didn't have to walk around the backside of the animals. One day, unexpectedly, just as I was walking under the neck of a cow, she jumped onto the edge of the manger with her chest and squashed my head firmly to the edge of the manger. A loud scream made the farmer come instantly to knock the cow off me. The cow did that because she was in heat. How was I to know? All the skin on the upper part of the right side of my face had been scraped off. A crust formed over it, and I had that crust for weeks. Then the teacher who had it in for me rubbed some cream from a tube on the crust, and soon after that, the crust came off in big chunks.

In the stable, there were two oxen that constantly faced one another. That caused them to get dirty on the front part of their bodies when they laid down to have a rest. Normally, the animals faced the manger and would only turn their heads to see to the left or right. Their shit would drop beyond the length of their bodies, and they wouldn't get dirty from it. Now I thought of finding a solution to this two constantly turning sideways. I tied their tails together. That seemed to function— except they both started to pull in the opposite direction, and the knot became extremely tight. Then I realized that Luis wouldn't agree with my experiment and was better if I undid the knot. Now the knot had become so tight that it took me ages to undo it.

In the home of the family, there was a small square mirror over the sink that also served as washbasin. It was big enough that I could see my face and not much more. Paul said one day, "What are you looking at?" "The mirror," I said. "Can I see it too?" he asked. "Yes, of course, you can." I lifted him high enough that he could see himself. This was the first time that he looked in a mirror and wouldn't believe that it was himself he saw in it.

Luis' father died. He died at home and was laid out in his room. For three days before his burial, an evening prayer was held every day. People from near and far away would come to pray for this dead man.

In October, it would be my tenth birthday. There wasn't any

point in looking forward to it because I knew that I wouldn't receive anything. I did receive free haircuts from Anna. She cut Luis' and Paul's hair as well.

Luis and I had a dispute, and I left to go home. On the way home, I went to see a farmer who had asked me in the past if I could go to work for him. I went to see if he was still interested. He said yes, but I wanted to go home first. I walked to get the train, but I didn't have the money for the train fare. Therefore, I waited a bit away from the station so that the station master wouldn't see me till the train came. Then when the train did come and had stopped, I ran up to it and went in without getting a ticket. On the train, I didn't sit on a third-class wooden seat but walked up and down the carriages and looked out from the windows. Then, when the ticket collector came and asked me for the ticket, I replied, "My parents have got it." He accepted that explanation and continued with his work. He must have seen that I was the only person that had got on that train at the last station. He probably felt sorry for me and let it go at that.

After I got home, my mother took me straight back to Luis, and after a long discussion with him, she left me there and told me to stay there. That was the last straw. I was big enough to earn my living. I was big enough to find myself a new job, and my own mother would humiliate me to that extent? In my heart, I have never forgiven her for that decision. I soon got over that humiliating experience, and life continued.

Now this family where I was staying at wanted me to look my best when I went to church on Sundays. They had a suit made for me. They said that I looked smart in it. Yes, I felt proud going to the village in my new suit. No one noticed that I had a new suit, but that didn't matter. The important part was that I thought that they noticed. I was wearing my first suit, which was made especially for me. People just had to notice my new suit.

The winter was a repeat of the previous year. I was kept from going to school just as much as the year before. I still had to take the milk to a family in the village on my way to school then go back to retrieve the milk can on my way home. Secretly, I liked Anneliese more and more. Smiles were exchanged on every occasion we got.

On a school day, the classes with the bigger children were taken to the forest, and we all got the job of planting small pine trees. We were shown what we had to do and how we had to do it. During a break, we were given a bite to eat and some fizzy orange. Getting the fizzy orange was a real treat for all. We all went back for a second helping.

The children at school started talking about the skiing race. It would be held on a Sunday afternoon. As they had spoken so much about the race, I went to see it. It was being held on some steep hills on the outskirts of the village. This was the first time that I watched a skiing race and the first time that I had seen a prepared slalom truck. I couldn't understand what all the poles were for until the race started. Then it became clear what they were for. This racing did look as if it was good fun, as the skier zigzagged from one side of one pole to the other side of the next pole, down all the slope.

This did look like such good fun that I decided to ask baby Jesus to bring skis for me at Christmas. I had to send a card to my mother so that she could tell baby Jesus what I liked for Christmas. My mother was the go-between, as I didn't have his address. Seeing that some of the boys that had taken part in the race were smaller than me, I thought I was surely big enough to take part in such a race too.

On another occasion, Luis and Anna took me to a prayer ceremony for someone who had died. I never met the person but had to go as well. As soon as I walked into that house, we entered a room filled with people. After a while, I felt strange in that crowded room. Some sort of cold feeling went through my body that made me feel strange, so strange that after a while, I thought I would lose my balance or faint. I managed to fight off the foreseen consequences of that falling and the fainting, but I was longing to get out of that place. As we eventually did get out, I started feeling better and better until that strange feeling passed.

Hay had to be collected from the hut in the Alps. Luis didn't have horses. Therefore, he at times arranged for others to collect it with horses, but on this occasion, he used his oxen. With a horse-drawn cart, one would sit on the cart and direct the horses with reins. They walked quicker than oxen did. Oxen had to be led by walking at the front of them when they pulled a cart. This took longer to walk all the way up to the Alps and back. The loading of the cart was quicker when it was done for horse because there were two men loading and me trampling the hay in the wagon. The loading for oxen took longer because it was only Luis loading the wagon and me trampling the hay. The journey up to the Alps and back took longer too with the oxen. Two oxen were stronger than one horse and never got stuck with a load in the swamps.

By Claudio Paterno

As the return journey was basically all downhill, one horse managed it without problems. In some places, the soil was wet and soggy. To make it easier for the horse, we would all help to push on the hay-loaded wagon. On this occasion, we saw some tourists on the Alps. They asked if they could take a photo of us. Luis said yes, and we felt both proud to have had our photo taken. Part of my working costume was an apron. To support the upper part of the apron, the ribbon was placed over the head and left to rest behind the neck. Then the apron was tied round the waist too. The space between the waist and up the front of the breast was used as a pocket. Normally, this pocket was just empty. Occasionally, food for my picnic was stored in it. For special occasions, some men had animals, flowers, or scenery embroidered on the part of the apron above the waist. At times, when needed, the bottom right corner would be lifted to the waist and tied there by pushing the corner under the band that was tied around the waist. It was easier to walk if one side of the apron was tied to the waist.

Ignaz informed me that Mario was getting married and that we could both go to the wedding. This was something new to look forward to. I imagined that there would have been loads of cakes and such like to eat, and orange juice to drink. When the time came to go, Ignaz was allowed to go, and I wasn't. The disappointments I was given on different occasions were stored inside me. I simply could not understand why, on the few hours I had off on a Sunday afternoon, I was not allowed to see my brother, Ignaz. Now, I was not allowed to go to my brother's wedding. I was never allowed to go on a school outing. Rather than giving me the money to participate at a school outing, Luis would keep me at home to work.

Then before the summer, I heard that my youngest brother had also been taken to a farm in this same area. The farm where he ended up was on the same street where Ignaz was. Only Claudio was further from the village than Ignaz. I was allowed to go to him just the once. At the farm where Claudio was, they were German-speaking, and they changed his name from Claudio to Klaus, a young man that had no nose. To see him left me with a strange feeling that I had not experienced before. Klaus looked ever so young to me to be working on a farm. Then, come to think of it, this was the fourth year that I was away from home, and Klaus was four years younger than me. Therefore, I, too, must have been as young when I started as he was. The farmers where Ignaz and I were were also German-speaking, but they didn't change our names from Italian to German.

The farms where Ignaz and Klaus were didn't have any pastures on the Alps. I was the only one of us three that would have gone to the Alps in the summer for a few months. That time of going to the Alps had come once more. This year, Maria and I didn't get on as well as we had done the year before. I simply couldn't understand why I was doing everything wrong from her point of view. I did what I had to do, just like I had done it the year before and the one before that.

When we left the Alps to return to Siusi, Luis started to have a go at me because of my behavior towards his mother. This was getting a bit much. The mother was causing problems and got her son to help her as well. I felt that the atmosphere had become unpleasant. I got dressed in my new suit, took my few things, and started to leave. Nothing had been said to me about payment; therefore, I didn't ask for any wages. Luis then said, "You are not going in that suit. That is staying here." I had to take it off and get dressed in my old best clothing. By now, it was a bit small for me, but I left, never to return.

When I got home, my mother wasn't at all pleased to see me.

## Chapter Eighteen

DURING THE TIME THAT I WAS IN SIUSI, in St Florian, a village close to Laghetti, a new water-driven power station was being built. Part of the works involved tunneling through the mountain to reach a lake at the very top. Unexpectedly, the tunneling hit an unknown underground lake, and the water gushed down the tunnel and simply couldn't be stopped. Now that I had come home, I could see that a wide part of the forest was missing, and only gravel could be seen in its place. Lodovico was working with the construction of the new power plant. To transport materials to the top of the mountain, a cable transport system was used.

That was where Lodovico worked. He worked on shifts, and I was asked to take Lodovico's lunch or dinner to him. The food was placed in a food Thermos-flask. The flask was placed in a bag, and I carried it, walking for twenty minutes one way to Lodovico. It was just Lodovico that used the bicycle to go to work. At times, I hitchhiked for the first thousand meters or so. If no one stopped by this time, I would just walk the rest of the way without holding up my thumb. Then, I had to wait for him to eat and bring back the flask and bag. On my return, I hitchhiked too. There was one occasion that I got a lift, and when I got to my destination, the driver said, "For this short distance, you hitchhiked!" On another occasion, a car stopped; and in the car, it stank of shit. I was pleased to get out of it. Then the next day, I noticed that it was me who had some excrement on my shoes. It was strange to feel embarrassed in retrospect. Normally, I felt embarrassed at the moment of a malfunction. But on this occasion, I felt embarrassed on the day after the unfortunate event.

At home, there was now one room just for Mario, and his wife, Gemma. I met Gemma, my sister-in-law, for the first time after I had come back from Siusi. We got on fine together. In October, before I returned to my old school, I helped Gemma's parents with the grape harvest. They had a grape plantation near Trento of different types of grapes. This was the last type of grape that was being harvested. To have harvested the grapes this late, they must have been a special sort of grape. Most grapes got harvested in September. Harvesting at different times for different wines is a possibility. For some wines, the grapes must get the frost before harvesting. I know that it was cold getting out in the grape pergolas. The sun took such a long time to get to us. First, it shined on the top of the mountains on the western side, and slowly, the shining got lower until it got to us. It still took some time before I felt the warmth of the sun. After this harvesting was finished, I returned to school in Laghetti.

With some subjects in this school, they were a long way ahead of Siusi. It took me some time before I caught up with the others. Except for reading. With that subject, I had accepted being the worst of the class wherever I was and in whichever school I went to. If the teacher hadn't asked me to read aloud, I wouldn't have felt embarrassed, and that made it even worse. Strange that the subject I was bad in was the subject that was done aloud. Mathematics, which I was good at, wasn't done aloud. With the other subjects at this school, I wished to be close to the top of the class. Here, the teacher commented and said, "How can you draw so well and have such bad handwriting?"

Drawing, I could understand, and I liked it, while writing was just a pain. I couldn't really understand the purpose of writing. I still couldn't read and understand the words. It took me so long to read a word that by the time I had read it, I had not understood its meaning. I simply could not understand how some people read ahead of the words. When some people read out aloud and misread a word, they went back several words to get to the misread word. Some people could pick up a book and not put it down until they finished reading it. If I had done that, I would have died from lack of sleep several weeks later.

Now, I also found out who it was that went to take my place in Aldagno. It was a boy from my class. On occasions, we spoke about the farm, the boys at the farm, and Nondel. The discussion about Nondel wasn't over in just five minutes. We discussed her on and off for several days. In the end, the other boy ended up with the nickname, Nondel. He was also there for one summer in Aldagno. We were both wondering where they would have got a boy to replace us after that.

At this school, there was Marlene that I liked best of all the girls, but my friend Roberto liked her too, and on top of that, she must have been the favorite for all the boys. We got on well together, and she always had a nice smile for me, which she received returned direct from my heart.

Ignaz and Klaus came home for Christmas. This time, we prepared some beds in the loft to have a sleeping place for everyone. Pino and I went to get a Christmas tree like we did some years ago. He had also bought some tree and crèche decorations and did most of the decorating for this event. The Christmas time passed with one more member in the family, my sister-in-law. We all liked her, and she joined in just like a family member. She had a brother who was a missionary in some foreign land, and another brother was at home with her parents.

Franz, my cousin, and Lodovico took Ignaz and me to Bolzano to see a film. This was the first time that I went to the cinema. I could see how full of smoke the cinema was. At that time, one could enter and exit at any time from the cinema we had gone to. In some cinemas, one was allowed to enter and exit at any time. We didn't get in at the beginning of the film and came out once it started to repeat itself. Franz and Lodovico left us in the cinema while they left for some time.

The festive period was soon over. Two brothers returned to Siusi, and all others continued with their normal routine.

During the carnival period, Roberto lent me a mask. It was a big mask that covered the body and had a face of some sort of historic animal. Walking in the village, people used to say, "Ah, that is Roberto with his mask." If they thought that I was Roberto, then I also had to change my voice. I couldn't copy his voice, but I could change mine so that they didn't recognize me. Oh yes! This was a chance to go and see what Marlene would say to Roberto. Unfortunately, Marlene wasn't at home. Her mother came to the door and spoke to me for a while, not knowing who I was. I could have been Roberto, but she couldn't be sure.

With the passing of time, Pino finished his apprenticeship and worked in Egna. That was the village after St Floriano. The company he worked for did plumbing, metal work, and glazing.

My mother ended up finding me a new farm job where I would work the following year. At least, this time, it was in my own village. At the beginning, I worked there in the daytime, and I went home to sleep. I would, on occasions, play cards with my mother. My mother taught me a few card games, and we played them at times.

The new farmer had a fruit plantation, grass, vegetables, and maize. He also had a horse and no other animals apart from cats and chickens. After a while of working with this farmer, Giovanni, I ended up sleeping at his place. Giovanni was married and had twins: a boy and a girl. They were about five years old. The boy became very attached to me, and I was fond of him. Often, he was next to me in the fields when I worked there.

The roads had roadside markers made of stone and painted white with a black stripe about one-third from the top. These markers were on both sides of the road. These roadside markers were good for nighttime driving.

One day, we were all in the fields, and something had been forgotten at home. I was asked to go and get it with the bike. The boy wanted to come too. He sat on the cross bar of the bike, and off we went. On the way, he did something, and we fell. He hit his head on one of these roadside markers, and he started bleeding. I continued with him and took him to an aunt of his in the village. While she bandaged him, I went to get the article that had been forgotten. Then

I went back to work and explained what had happened and said where the boy was. They were a bit angry that I had taken the boy on the bike. The farmer's wife, Silvia, often left before Giovanni and me, and she went home with the bike to prepare the dinner. This time, she left to go and see how the boy was and to take him home. By the time Giovanni, his daughter, and I got home, the boy had a bandage on his head but was fine. That experience was a shock that I will not forget.

The lady here cooked the best omelets I had ever eaten. She often cooked omelets for the evening meal, and I absolutely loved them. I worked on this farm until the harvesting was finished, and the cabbages were sliced, prepared, and placed in the butt to become sauerkraut. In the spring and early summer, I would guide the horse in between the rows of grapes and apple trees. The horse was pulling a cart with a big wooden barrel on it, which was just like a wine barrel. The barrel would be filled with some sort of liquid that would be sprayed on the plants or injected into the soil. When it was injected into the soil, Giovanni used a big syringe (injection tool). With the foot, he would push it into the soil and inject some of the liquid into it. The cart had a motor on it and a pump that would apply some pressure on the liquid being pumped. Whether it was pumped or sprayed, by the time we had gone down one lane in between the trees and came back on the next lane to where we had started, we could see the difference in color of the trees that had been done at the beginning and the ones that still had to be done. The color of the trees that had been done at the beginning was much greener and were a dark green. The same thing happened when the trees were sprayed with the specially prepared liquid. At the return from the round trip, the difference was really noticeable. I was surprised to see how quickly the liquid was absorbed by the roots of the trees and taken to the leaves to make them change color.

Giovanni had one field with corn. The field was near a small lake, and the soil was just sand. Working this sandy soil was a lot easier than working the heavy soil. At first, the field was plowed. After this, rows were formed, and maize was sown by hand. Just a few grains were sown at an approximated distance of about twenty to thirty centimeters. When the grain started to grow, it had to be thinned out. I was shown how this had to be done. With a hoe, I had to eliminate the plants that were too close to one another. There had to be just one maize plant every thirty centimeters. After this, very little had to be done to this grain until the harvesting. It grew fast and tall. It was so tall that I could walk in between the rows, and no one would see me. The same happened to a grown-up as well.

With the harvesting, Silvia helped as well. The plants had two to three lots of ears on them. They had to be broken off and placed on a sack, which I had around my shoulder. The sack was then emptied into a big container each time I got to the end of a row. The container looked like a big half of a rugby ball cut in halves longways and was made of stems of a special bush. At the end of the day, the maize was taken home and was then unloaded by tipping the container sideways, just where Giovanni wanted it. In the evenings, some villagers, including Marlene, would gather. They would find a convenient place to sit for them to open the leaves on the ears and remove some of them. After a while of working, there were so many leaves around each person that one couldn't find the ears. A few leaves were left on each ear so that it could be tied into a bundle of about twenty ears. The bundles would then be placed over a wire to dry in a ventilated area.

These drying areas were the favorite areas for the sparrows, and it was just impossible to keep them out. All sorts of solutions were tried to keep them out but only had partial success. Later in the autumn or winter, the grains were removed from the ears and taken to the mill to be ground into flour. This was consequently used for the most important food consumption of that area. The cooked flour was called polenta. The polenta was constantly stirred while it was cooking and then poured onto a flat wooden tray which normally was on the table. Now each person at the table would take a part of the polenta and place it on their own plate. This was done in different ways by different families. Some would use a knife to cut it and would use the same knife as a pallet to transport it to their plate. Others used a string to cut it and a pallet to take it from the flat board and place it onto their plate. Anything could be eaten with it. In fact, it was more conventional than potatoes or pasta. When on the plate, it could be eaten just like potatoes with cheese, sausages, goulash, and such like. But when it was cold, the children loved it sliced just like bread and sprinkled with sugar, covered in jam, with some sliced sausages or cheese. At times, I had it with warm milk for breakfast.

During this summer, on Sundays, some boys went to the village bar-restaurant to watch TV. Yes! In the village, there was the very first black and white TV, and the boys went to watch it. A series, "Maschera di Zorro," was being shown at that time on Sunday afternoon.

Also, a small circus came to the village. It was a family circus with parents and a beautiful daughter. The display was in the open, and people made donations. The circus was there for two weeks and always gave the same display. I liked to go to it because it became like a village gathering. The daughter in her different costumes was so beautiful that the young men simply couldn't take their eyes off her. After the two weeks, the circus left. Some years later, I heard that the village idiot (as he was called) married the circus beauty. The young men from the village talked for years about the event of the village idiot marring that beauty.

## Chapter Nineteen

I BECAME UNCLE TO ROSALBA. Rosalba was Mario's first child, and she was a girl. To me, she was a normal newborn baby, but they all said what a beautiful baby she was. Grown-ups always said that about small babies. To me, my first niece became interesting when she started to walk and speak. When she was a bit bigger, at times, she sat on my lap and fed me at meal times. Then, with my teeth, I would hold the fork or spoon that she used to feed me with, and she would tell me to stop it.

I went to school during the week, but on Saturdays, I could work in the workshop where Pino was working. There, I had to clean machinery and the workshop. At lunchtime, we went to the boss' house for lunch, and in the evening, as I was about to go home, I received 500 Lire. This was my first payment for a day's work. In the workshop, there was a machine that shaped the sheet metal into guttering. It had three round steel bars that had to be cleaned. I had to rub the round bars with fine sandpaper. Then, when I thought that I had finished them, from the boss' point of view, I had just started.

The workshop was opposite the school in the village center. Occasionally, a client would come into the shop, but the vast majority of the work was done out on-site. This company consisted of the boss, Paul Walter, and two professional operators. That was Pino and Karl. Karl came from Cortaccia, a village from the other side of the river. He had a motorbike and came to work with that bike. Pino had his own bicycle, which he used to go to work with. To go there on Saturdays, I used the family bike. We had school five days a week, but the workers had to work six days a week. At times, I was asked to help one of the two skilled workers. Here, they made metal guttering from galvanized sheeting. Then, I was also shown how to treat the guttering and change its appearance to a honey color.

It was a double operation. The first operation was to clean the gutters with some acid, and when they were dry, I had to treat them with an oil that would harden and give them a honey color. These gutters were as long as the machine could make them. The sections were cut from big sheets with a big guillotine cutter. They were reduced to the size required and made into whatever was needed. The boss had a 500cc motorbike with sidecar. With that sidecar, one of the three grown-ups would take the materials to the jobs, wherever they were needed. The longest articles they had to carry were six-meter galvanized water pipes. At both ends of the pipes on the side car, a warning plate was fixed to them, a plate with diagonal stripes in red and white to warn others of the danger.

I was also shown how to replace or fit a pane of glass to a window and how to repair a saucepan that had a hole in it. Replacing a pane of glass was, at times, a bit tricky. The old broken glass and putty had to be removed. Then, to remove the old putty, I had to use a special knife, hitting it from the back with a hammer. Sometimes the grain of the wood was obstinate, and it was difficult to get the old putty removed from it. I had also learned how to cut and fit a pane of glass. When I was learning, at times, I heard the experts say to the client, "You can't expect the glass to hold the frame together. Get something done about the frame and come again."

Once, when we went for lunch at Paul Walter's home, Pino showed me what the boss' dog could do. The boss' home was on the side of a river. Pino took a stone, spat on it, showed it to the dog, and let it sniff it. Then, Pino threw it into the river, where the water was thirty to forty centimeters deep. The dog would run after the stone and jump in the river, and even under water, he found the very same stone that Pino had thrown in. He would bring it and would give it to Pino. He did it several times, and the dog always came back with the same stone. The dog loved that game, but our lunch break had a time limit.

Once, I had to help Karl fit guttering on a roof of a big fruit storage hall. I had to lie on the roof, which had a slight slope, and hold the sections of guttering while Karl soldered them to the previous section that had been fixed. From lying still on that roof and holding the freezing guttering, my hands got frozen. I was beginning to realize that this job wasn't for me when I left school.

There were other times and other aspects of the job which, at times, I liked. Like plumbing was better than sheet metal work. Okay, the grown-ups did the easy part of the job while I had to cut the pipes from measurements I received, and then I had to cut a thread at either end of the pipe. Prepare the correct amount of hemp, wrap it round the thread of the pipe, and paint linseed oil over the hemp. Once the pipe was completed, I had to take it to whoever had asked for it. At times, the part I had prepared was the wrong measurement, and I had to do it all over again. This time with the correct measurements. I felt that they did it deliberately to give me a wrong measurement to observe my reaction. Had they given it to me in writing, I could have seen who made the mistake. This way, it was their word that counted, and they were always right.

This year, I could participate in all events arranged at school. Once, the teacher arranged an outing just for her class. On another occasion, the school arranged an outing for all the school children. We all took a picnic from home. My mother had prepared a cake and had packed a piece with my picnic. Receiving cake was a yearly treat to be remembered for life.

The vicar also arranged an outing for a Sunday afternoon. He, with the youth of the village, took us to San Genesio. It was a village above Bolzano, and we went up the hill by cable car. On the plains of San Genesio, there were games held with participants from many villages. One of the events was a run around a big field, and the winner would receive a watch. I was extremely tempted to participate. Then I was a bit embarrassed to participate. I just didn't know how good the others were. Then when they eventually started, I couldn't believe that they didn't run any faster. When I was chasing the cows, I must have run a lot faster than this. Now I was really sorry that I didn't participate and win that watch I so desired.

Back at school, I really liked Marlene more and more. I never met Marlene alone outside the school times. Despite that, her gentle manner and lovely smile entered deeply into my heart.

All the cooking at home was done with a wood-burning stove; therefore, wood was needed all year and had to be sawn and chopped to the size that would fit in the stove. Some candling wood was also needed to light the fire with. The bundles from the grape vines didn't last all year. I did this wood cutting quite regularly. When the sawn timber was in big chunks, I could simply set it on the chopping block, and it would stay upright by itself. Then when the logs were smaller, at times, they wouldn't stand upright by themselves, and I had to hold them. I would hold them with my left hand and use the ax with my right hand.

One time, I held the log, and for some unknown reason, I had my thumb on top of the log and ended up hitting it with the ax. It cut about half of the nail off. Seeing the blood, I got a shock, and instead of going indoors using the back door, I ran to the front door and went to my mom. She pushed the part back that was still hanging on the thumb and bandaged it.

The following day, it started to hurt more and more. Two days later, my hand was swollen and was truly painful. Then the day after that, my mother said I should go to Bolzano to the doctors. I cycled to Bolzano and found the medical office where she told me to go. After waiting and waiting in a queue until it was my turn, they started to ask questions. Like: Was I working when it happened? Of course, I was working; otherwise, it wouldn't have happened. Well, in that case, I had to go to this office for accidents that happened at work. "How could my mother have made such a mistake?" was the question in my mind.

Anyway, I went to this other office, and after waiting once more in an endless queue, they asked for my work insurance number. I didn't know what that was, let alone have one. Now here they asked, too, "Where did it happen?" This time, I said, "I was chopping firewood at home, and while I was doing that, I cut my thumb."

"Well, in such a case, you have to go to this medical office." They gave me the same name as my mother had given me. I replied, "I have just come from this place, and they said to me to come here." "Well, they shouldn't have. They should have seen from your age that you were still at school."

Back in the other medical center, I waited in that endless queue once more while the pain was hammering at my arm. When it was eventually my turn to see the interviewer, I had to explain that I was working at home and not for an employer when the accident happened. By now, the upper part of my hand was so swollen that the doctor made a cut in it, and with tweezers, he pulled out strings of pus that had a long root on them. He medicated and bandaged it and gave me a sling that held my arm against my chest. Now I had to cycle home holding the handlebar with just one hand. As the pain was easing, I used both hands on the handlebar.

It was normally dangerous enough cycling on these roads. Many lorries had trailers on them, which made them ever so long in total. On these winding roads, one had to be ever so careful. Despite that, I was cycling on the extreme edge of the road. I had once been caught by part of a trailer, and it pulled me off the road and into the ditch. How could the driver see what happened so far back from him? Fortunately, I wasn't hurt, but I could have been in that ditch until the next cyclist had come along. A car driver wouldn't have seen me. Now by having experienced what pain was, I was even more concerned about avoiding an accident.

Ignaz had also come home for good from Siusi. I assume that the children from where he was in Siusi had grown big enough to do what Ignaz had done. One day, the two of us were digging in the rough ground of our property for some reason. While digging, we ended up uncovering a rotten part of a tree. As a joke, Ignaz said, "Look, we found gold, gold, gold." He said it loud enough that the neighbors heard him. They came running to see what we had found. I didn't see what it had to do with them, but they weren't pleased about this misleading event.

Sometime later, Ignaz and I walked to my godmother's house, which was reasonably close. It was dark as we walked home. Then I heard a thud. It was a stone that had hit Ignaz on the head and caused him to bleed. I often wondered if that stone was in any way related to the innocent joke.

Later, Ignaz started a butcher apprenticeship in Trento. He would often come home on Sundays and would bring whatever meat the boss gave him to take home.

At school, two other boys and I arranged to go to the Garda lake with our bikes on Sunday. We wanted an early start and were to meet in the village at five. I went to the meeting place at five and waited and waited. After about half an hour, I left and started the journey by myself. It was seventy kilometers to get to the Garda lake. I had planned to do a round trip, which I ended up doing. Down on one road and back on another road. From Trento, the road went uphill and was quite hard going. Then it changed, and it became a gentle downhill cycling for most of the way. I went to the lake and had a picnic. After having looked around for a while in Garda, I started my way back. Now, I got to Torbole, and seeing that I was there, I had to see some of that place too. Then from Torbole, it went steep uphill. Fortunately, it was for a short distance. After which, it was on the level nearly all the way.

When I got to Trento, I felt that I still had time to see Ignaz. I went to see him, and together, we went to the cinema. After having seen the film, I continued my way home. Now I realized that I should never have stopped for so long in Trento. The rest of my way home was pure punishment. There were still thirty-one kilometers left to do, and they seemed to never end. A slight panic set in. I didn't know if I would make it as far as home. I didn't know that I had so many muscles in my body that could ache so much. It took twice as long to do this last thirty kilometers than what I had reckoned with.

On the following day at school, I asked the other two why they didn't come to Garda lake. They replied, "We didn't think that you really meant it."

As spring slowly arrived, I started to wear shorts and short-sleeved shirts. I also used the bicycle to go to school. This was good fun. As my home was higher up from the main road, there was a downhill slope to the main road. From the top of the slope, I could listen if there was traffic coming from either way. If it was silent, I would let the bike go as fast as it could. Then when I got to the main road, I had to turn left, which became a work of art at that speed. Well, one day, I hadn't heard a scooter. We got to the same spot at the same time. By trying to avoid it, I ended up extremely close to a roadside stone and hit it with my right leg. The scooter driver didn't stop, despite living just a few hundred meters from where I was sitting in pain.

In pain, I managed to get up and go to school. I then noticed that, during the day, my right leg was getting blue and black. Now I was also scared of receiving a hiding at home. They constantly told me that I wasn't to cycle down that hill at top speed and not observe the give way on the main road. My biggest thought was, "How I could explain at home how it happened?" What could I say? Apart from the pain, I had this problem as well. When the time came to go home, I couldn't bend my right knee. It was so painful that I had to keep it straight. I ended up peddling the bike with my left leg. When I got home, I entered quietly, went to my room, and changed my shorts for long trousers.

Well, that did hide my discolored leg, but it didn't hide my limping. I managed to hide my limping for a while. I hadn't thought that my cousins would have told at their home about my accident. After a few weeks, my grandmother came to see us, and she asked how my leg was. By now, the limping had got better, but the leg was still black from top to bottom. After so much time had passed between the accident and my mother hearing about it, she expressed her concern verbally and not physically with a branch from a weeping willow. Besides, I had nearly become a man, compared to the time I wet the bed, and I could have taken the whipping weapon from her.

## Chapter Twenty

AT HOME, THE WATER SHORTAGE PROBLEM had to be seen to. The water came from a lake high up in the mountain. From there, it went to the village, which was lower than my home. As the villagers used the water more and more for watering the gardens and fields, the water simply didn't arrive at my house. On occasions, at night, we did manage to fill some buckets, but that didn't last for long. As our neighbor pumped water from the ground, we thought of doing the same. As we were somewhat higher in altitude, Pino and I had to dig a hole for a well. Apparently, the pumps managed to suck the water only from so many meters down and pushed it a lot higher than it could suck it from.

We excavated the hole six meters deep, and after that, we hammered a specially prepared pipe into the ground. This pipe was ten centimeters in diameter with a specially prepared point at the front and had holes in it for the first part of its six-meter length. The inside of the pipe remained virtually empty as it entered the ground. A tripod was prepared with a wheel at the top and had a rope placed over it. The rope was used to pull the weight that hammered the pipe into the ground. When the pipe was halfway into the ground, starting from six meters below ground level, we couldn't resist lowering a string with a weight on it, down the pipe to see if it would get wet. This procedure was repeated more and more often as the pipe entered deeper into the ground.

The pipe had to have a second pipe fitted to it. When the full length of the second pipe entered the ground, there was water inside it. Twelve meters of pipe to reach the water was the limit of the sucking capacity of the pump. Therefore, we had to dig the hole deeper to ease the strain on the pump and to make sure that it would supply the water so badly needed. We dug the hole deeper and made a concrete platform for the pump to rest on. We also lined the sides of the hole with concrete to make it safe in the well. After that, all the piping had to be done from the water to the pump and from the pump to the kitchen. The pipe to the water had a one-way valve fitted to it. The water could enter the pipe but could not exit the pipe at its base. This way, the pump was constantly primed once it was filled at the beginning. After electricity was connected to the pump, it was tested, and it functioned. Yes, this was an electric pump and not a manually operated one, like the neighbors' pump that I used when the house was being built.

At the beginning, there was a lot of chalk in the water. The pump was left to run for a long time to extract the chalk from the surrounding area where the water came from. The pump was finally stopped, and the next time it was turned on, it didn't function. It had to be primed again. Now we could prime it with the water that it had pumped itself, which we stored in buckets. Then the next time it was turned on, the same thing happened. The conclusion was that grit had been trapped in the no-return valve. The pipe that went from the pump into the water had to be removed and pulled up to clean the valve. After this, the pump functioned perfectly, and we didn't have to go to our neighbor to get water and pump it by hand.

While working on this, I learned something new. Pino got some juice from the pantry to prepare some drinks. Then he nearly filled a glass bottle with water from the well and poured some juice into the water bottle. I was surprised to see that the color of the juice stayed on top of the water. Pino turned the bottle to make the juice and water mix. He then explained to me that the warm liquid was lighter than the cold liquid, and therefore, the juice stayed on top of the cold water. Of course, the juice from the larder was a lot warmer than the water that came from underground.

Another thing I couldn't understand was that, from the main road, there was an excavation into the hillside. At the top of the excavation and some thirty meters back from the edge, there was the new well, which was next to my home. The face of the excavation was a lot higher than the depth of where the water was. If we found water at about five meters above the base of the excavation, why didn't the water come out from the side of the excavation? I simply couldn't understand why the water didn't seep out from the side of the excavation if it was higher than the bottom of it.

One day, when Pino and I took a break from working on the well, he turned on the radio, and at that moment, the report about the brand new FIAT 500 was being transmitted. So, the two-seater Topolino car was being replaced with the new 500. That was the first time that I had heard such a report, and there were a lot of the technical details I didn't understand. Pino explained some of them to me but not all of them. In any case, I found it fascinating that so much could be said about a car. Then when the price was said, we realized that even small cars were only for rich people.

On a Sunday, Pino went to Egna and returned with a girlfriend of his and her younger sister, Olga. At one point, we all went for a walk to the forest. After a while, we separated into pairs. Pino walked away with his girlfriend while I was left with Olga. She was very close to my age and very pretty. We walked alone for a while. Then we sat on the ground and chatted about the novelty of us being alone. This was the first time I found myself in such a situation with a girl. She talked about her stockings and showed me how high they went and how they were held up. This was so new to me that I didn't know what to say or which way to look. I felt embarrassed while she seemed to be so natural. For me, it simply wasn't natural to see where the stockings ended on a girl's legs. She must have noticed that I was blushing and changed conversation. But now, she pulled her knees up so that her loose skirt slid down the upper part of her legs as far as it would go by itself. I felt that there was an open offer for me to take it further, and I was simply too inexperienced and too shy to do anything about it.

After a while, I heard Pino calling us. We got up and walked towards the other two. I had been dreaming for a long, long time to have a sexual experience with a nice girl like Olga, and now I let my chance escape. In those days, it was virtually forbidden to talk about sex. I only spoke about sex with boys I knew, who were of approximately my age. Generally, it was simply forbidden by the families for girls to have sex before marriage. Even for boys, or at least in my case, one couldn't mention the word sex at home. I was actually led to believe that girls only had sex to please the boys. It took me some years to learn that ladies could obtain pleasure from sex as well as men. Up to then, I really thought that ladies only did it to please men. Religion and lack of general information had a lot to do with my ignorance. There was absolutely nothing to be seen or heard about sex. There was a total lack of sexual education. It was a sin to even think about it.

The villagers had a custom wherein the eighteen-year-olds would all together on the same day for the military medical test. For this occasion, they would decorate a cart, which would be drawn by a horse. It became decorated with tree branches and flowers. It had openings in it, just like open windows. These young men also had decorated hats. For weeks in advance of the medical test, they would make themselves heard in the streets of the village by singing. They would also go up the bush forest to a rock way above the village. From here, with a megaphone, they would call out aloud for the villagers to hear a phrase, something like, "On this date and on this earth, a lovely girl got married. Who is she? Who is she not? Then they would say her name. Whom did she marry? Whom did she not marry? She married John Blogs." This way, all young ladies from the village got paired off with the most unexpected man one would have thought of. Then, when the day came for the medical test, these young men could do nearly anything and get away with it. It didn't matter how the medical test went in Trento. By the time they returned, there wouldn't be one single one of them that was still a virgin. A few years later, the brothels were eliminated in Italy. After this event, the group of each year would regularly meet up once a year with the ladies of the same age and have an outing.

In Laghetti, only the Nicoletti family had a car. It was a four-seater FIAT, used as an unofficial taxi service, and in emergencies, as an ambulance too. That family had four sons and one daughter. The second oldest son, Enzo, was ever so helpful in emergency cases. The youngest son, Ricardo, was about my age, and we went to school together. Carlo, the third oldest, went to school with Pino.

At that time, that family had the monopoly on groceries in the village, owning the only grocery store. They had the only petrol station and the only hotel. They had a bar too, but it wasn't the only bar in the village. Then, bit by bit, the competition started. One person opened a cheese shop from his home. Another family opened a grocery shop. Then another family built a big hotel. Anyway, it was a big hotel for the area. Now the hotel war got started. The Nicoletti family made their original hotel bigger and built one about a thousand meters on the other side of the Monti Hotel.

The hotels were a God-send for the young men of the village. As tourism became more and more popular, more and more cars and coaches would stop at the hotels with lovely young foreign ladies. The young men from the village would hover by the hotels during the evening hours to see which hotel received the best-looking ladies to be talked about the next day. As they only stopped over for one night, the talk of the young men was about what nearly happened with the blonds who came from the north. I was old enough to understand but still too young to participate in this eventful and frustrating experience the young men went through. When they talked about it, in retrospect, it was always, "You went off with the nice blond that I liked." Or, "I do wish that I had spoken better German." Not all the young men were bilingual. Some had gone to Italian school and had German lessons. The German they knew was, by far, inferior to the others who had gone to German school and had Italian lessons. Italian was spoken in the village; therefore, it was learned automatically by all villagers.

My mother used to go to see her uncle, Peter, and his wife, Marta, in Innsbruck once a year. This uncle Peter had a daughter

I had never met, but my mother spoke often about her. I had met Peter and Marta when they came to Italy and had come to the Alpi di Siusi. My mother stayed in Innsbruck for about two weeks then returned to take care of the boys. This time, she was gone during the time that the well was being constructed. She returned to find running water in the kitchen once more.

*(Fabio at a tender age)*

Because of shortage of work, I was asked not to return to work. Pino continued working there. I ended up working for a bricklayer-tiler called Mario. He did a bathroom right next to the school in Egna. One day, he told me to prepare some sand mixed with cement and water. He said how moist it had to be and how much I had to carry up the outside stairs to the first floor, then he left for business purposes. I prepared the screed mix and carried it to the first floor with one bucket in each hand. As it was a big bathroom, this job seemed never ending. It felt as if my arms were getting longer and longer. As this day didn't seem to end, I ended up filling the buckets less and less as my legs were getting wobbly, and my arms were nearly touching the ground. Working ten hours a day was normal for this time of year. At 100 Lire per hour, I would be getting 1,000 per day. Then, I used part of it for my lunch.

The evening came, and the boss didn't come to use the mix I had carried to the bathroom. That I found most annoying. All my hard work had to be done all over again. I was old enough to understand that he got a payment for materials, and he had used a part of it to go and have a nice time instead of working and using the mix that was waiting for him. Then, on the next day, the mix was hard and had to be thrown out. In lumps, it had to be taken to the balcony and thrown to the ground. Now he helped me with the new mix and with the initial carrying of the mix to the bathroom. Once he had sufficient mix to work with, he started to spread it and level it. Then he started to lay the floor tiles on it. I had to continue carrying the mix to the bathroom until Mario finished the job. As the school was next to this job, I was eyeing up a school girl who had caught my eye. She was at school for the last year.

While the boss waited for the newly laid floor tiles to harden on the cement, we went to another job. This job was in a village called Ora. Here, he had another bathroom to do. This, too, was on the first floor of an older building. Here, I had to clear out some debris and clean the place. The bathroom had a window with a fig tree right close to it. In fact, I could reach the branches from the window, and the nice big brown figs were just irresistible. . Once I finished my job, I made an attempt at reaching a fig on the tree. They were just a bit too far away. I ended up standing on the windowsill and reaching for that fig. At that moment, the property owner saw me from the garden, and he became raving mad. I retreated from my position, half-in and half-out of the window. The owner came to me with a whip and was absolutely out of his mind.

I went to find Mario. He was in a bar in Egna. I told him to find a replacement because I had enough of this treatment. First, he got me to work like a slave, taking the mix to the first floor for nothing, and now this behavior from a grown-up. He did calm me down and took me back to the job. There, he spoke to the owner and asked me if I had 1,000 Lire. "Yes," I said. "Well, give it to me," he said. I gave him that money, which he then gave to the owner of the property. On Saturday, I assumed that Mario would have given it back to me with my wages. That wasn't so. Therefore, I asked about it. He replied, "That was to calm Bruno about you being on the fig tree." So that cost me ten hours work for one fig.

After work, I made a point of trying to contact the girl who had caught my eye. I ended up meeting her, and her name was Carla. After work, we met nearly every day. We weren't alone; there was Lino from Laghetti and his friend, who was a girl from Egna. The four of us passed the evenings together until late. My mother started complaining that I didn't come home straight from work. So for her, it should have been all work and no pleasure. The pleasure we had was totally innocent. We probably went to the cinema or cycled to another village.

Enzo Nicoletti was having a new hotel built and a new petrol station next to the new hotel. One day, he simply came to my home and asked me to go and help the bricklayer working on his new project. Okay, I thought, that was no problem. I went there and took the orders from the bricklayer. At the end of the week, I went to see Enzo for my pay. "Ah," he said, "just keep a record of the hours you have worked." After about two months, Enzo asked me for the hours. Ten hours a day, six days a week for two months are 480 hours. It seemed a lot of hours to him, but he didn't pay me. A few days later, he asked me how many hours the bricklayer had worked. "Well, he worked the same hours as I had" was my reply. I continued to work at this new hotel.

After the work at the new power station was finished in St Florian, Lodovico was laid off. Therefore, he made a contract to go to work in Germany. Then Lodovico came home from Germany, and my hours and pay were discussed with Lodovico. I never saw a Lira for the work that I had done there. I never knew what agreement was reached between the two of them. After I finished the job at the hotel, I gave him the rest of my hours. These were more hours than the first lot. "I'll speak to your brother," he replied and took the hours from me. After this, Lodovoco left for a second contract in Germany.

*Years later, when talking to Lodovico about me having worked at Enzo's hotel with the bricklayer, he confirmed that he only discussed the first lot of 480 hours I had worked there. The money was, in fact, used to reduce the debt on the grocery shopping book. So, a son of the richest family of the village diddled me out of more than 500 hours of hard work.*

## Chapter Twenty-One

MY MOTHER STARTED TO DO a washing service for the Custom officers who were based in Egna. They came once a week to collect their whiter-than-white shirts, which they had brought the week before, and bring the used ones to be washed. Then after a while, she probably found it heavy going and stopped doing it.

The family orchard had been let on a fifty-fifty basis to a local farmer. The thing was that my father received whatever the farmer paid, and the family never had any benefit from it. Somehow, my mother persuaded my father to sell it and transfer the house into the name of the five boys still at home. My brother, Mario, had a share spent on him for the flat. Therefore, my parents thought that the naked property was worth about five times more than what Mario had received. Naked house is an expression used when a property is donated with the condition that the original owners can have the full benefit of the property for the rest of his or their lives. My mother received the money from the orchard, and she took care of it as she thought appropriate.

With the poverty and food shortage, I couldn't understand why this orchard was mainly used to grow grapes instead of growing food. Grapes probably produced more money. But what good is money if one is dying of hunger. I must admit that the only corn I have seen grown in the base of the valleys was, in fact, maize. Seeing that the flour from maize was the main substance for the local dish, I asked myself why that wasn't grown instead of grapes.

At home, I seldom saw my father, and my mother ended up having men friends. So much so that, at times, it was embarrassing even for me. When I was younger, a stranger who had a scooter brought her to see Ignaz and me. Now she had a new friend, the worst of the bad that she could have had.

I'll never forget Antonio Labate, a determined, bossy, olive-colored man that I simply couldn't take to. His wife lived in Bolzano and knew about this relationship. I didn't know what sort of relationship it was that my mother had with this man. I just knew that he was there to be the boss over everything. He did have a Vespa scooter, and he taught me to drive it. He also taught me to reline the clutch with slices of cork. That was cheaper than buying new clutch plates, and they lasted a few months. Teaching me that was the only thing he did that I liked. The stories he had were simply incredible— about the men he beat up, and only God knows what else.

This situation was getting a bit much for me, and I stayed away from home as much as possible. I went home to sleep, and that was about it. One day, I was allowed to drive the scooter to the local shop. The police were standing about ten meters past the entrance to the shop and waiting for someone to come along that they could wave down. As I arrived, they waved me down with their pallets, which they normally stuck in the side of their boots, held in the hand. I stopped by the shop, which was where I wanted to stop anyway. As they were a few meters further along, they wanted to know why I stopped off before I got to them. I said that I was going to the shop, and it wasn't my fault if they were a few meters further away. The cars and lorries were few in those days. Therefore, when I came with the scooter, they gave me a fine. I never did discover what the fine was for. They took every Lira I had on me. On having lost all my savings, I lowered my head in tears and returned home.

Close to my home, there was some building construction taking place. For this reason, there were lorries driving in and out of a side street. During the afternoon, I had driven to the village and had noticed that the road was wet from the lorries exiting the side road. When I returned in the evening, the scooter started to slide from side to side. I suddenly remembered that the wet on the road had become ice. As a lorry coming towards me was getting closer and closer, I threw myself in the ditch to avoid the lorry. This was the identical spot where I had the bike accident. Fortunately, this time, I wasn't hurt, and the scooter only had the front lightly damaged. The lorry driver saw what had happened and didn't stop to see if I had been hurt.

One Sunday during the summer, I went on my bike to see my brother, Klaus, in Siusi. After Bolzano, the road started to go uphill and never seemed to end. As a bonus, I would come down this very same road in the afternoon. Klaus was fine, and we both had a stroll in Siusi for a while before I started my return. While I was there, I was thinking about Anneliese, that girl who was so nice to me. On my way back, I stopped in Bolzano and had a look at the town. Well, there were places that I had heard about and had never seen. So, I was strolling in the town, partly cycling and partly walking, and came by the cathedral. To see it, well, I got off my bike and had a look around inside and outside. Right next to the cathedral was the post office. A man stood by the open door and started to make conversation with me. He seemed pleasant, and I liked his conversation. He said how boring it was to be working on a Sunday since people didn't come to the post office on Sundays. After a while, he invited me to the bar for a soft drink. He locked the post office door, and we went to the bar for a while. Here, he spoke about opening the post office on Sundays. I understood that it was only an experiment to open on a Sunday. Then he spoke about his family and that he had a daughter of about my age. This sounded interesting to me.

From here, I still had thirty kilometers to cycle home; therefore, I had to leave. I left this man, whose name was Bruno, with the promise that I would keep in touch. By the time I got home, it was really late, and my mother was concerned about me. Antonio was there too, and he had to have his say as well. Why I was so late was the question. (To be honest, I never gave it a thought that someone, including my mother, would have been concerned at what time I would have gotten home. I never said how long for I would have stayed with Klaus. I was concerned about getting home because

I had to get up in the morning.) After they constantly asked questions, in the end, I did say that I had stopped in Bolzano and that I had met this nice man. Well, me saying that was the biggest mistake I could have made. Antonio immediately accused him of being a homosexual who wanted more than to just buy me a soft drink. He insisted that I should admit that he tried something that he shouldn't have. This pressure was on me for about two weeks before Antonio eventually gave up his endless insistence that this man did or wanted to do more than just buy me a soft drink.

After some time, Bruno did write to me and asked that we should meet in Egna. With the pressure that was placed on me, I ended up having some doubts about initiating a friendship with Bruno and ignored his writing despite the fact that he had a daughter of about my age. Well, I hadn't seen his daughter, but if he was nice, I thought that she would have been nice too. I didn't know what a homosexual was, but after Antonio's reaction, I guessed what a homosexual was. I had never really experienced someone being nice to me in a personal way. All through my tender years, I was treated like a thing, an object, a slave that had to earn his living and never received a caress or even a nice word from anybody. The nearest I got to it was when I was really small, and my father would sit me on his knee and rub his week-old beard stubble on my face.

Now I was also developing sexually, and the thought of knowing a nice man, who most probably had a nice daughter, was most pleasing to me. The fact that I wasn't allowed to choose my own friends was somewhat disturbing to me. Well, I didn't like Antonio, and now I liked him even less. I just had the feeling that he shouldn't have been at my home so much, simply to take my father's place. As far as I was concerned, he could live in sin while I wasn't allowed to choose my friends.

This was also the era of the purple heart. For some years, a lot was said about the purple heart tablets. As far as I had understood, this was a tablet that stimulated and increased the normal performance of a person. I had heard that some cyclists used it to give better results. These tablets caused enormous scandals by people abusing them. A local story was spreading that two lady tourists enticed a young man to their tent. After overdosing him with purple heart, he was found dead the next day, and the ladies had gone. There was an article in the weekly paper about this incident. All grown-ups were asking, "What is this purple heart?" The young people didn't ask because they should have known what purple heart was. The stories about what purple heart was or must have been were just endless.

Antonio had his son at a collage somewhere in the Trento region. I was alone at home on this Sunday afternoon when Antonio came with his son, and he presented him to me as Antonino. We didn't have a bathroom, and therefore, I was told to get some water in the bowl. We did have a bowl for washing one's feet and a bigger one still for sitting in to have a wash. Well, I did get some water in the bowl him. "Now place it on the floor by the chair," Antonio said. No problem, I thought. His son sat on the chair and placed his feet in the water. Then Antonio insisted that I should wash Antonino's feet. I walked out the door and went to the forest. From there, I could see when they left for home. After they had gone, I was able to return. Now I was beginning to understand why the southern Italians were badly spoken about in the north of Italy.

A time came when there was no one at home except my mother and me. Mario had moved to Bolzano. Lodovoco went to work in Germany. Pino was away too. Ignaz was in Trento. Therefore, I was the only male at home. Antonio turned up one evening and started an argument with me about not obeying his commands. To which I replied, "I am not your son's servant." At that point, he grabbed my shirt and tried desperately to pull me out of the front door. I placed one hand on each side of the door frame, and he simply couldn't pull me any further. He knew the law, and he knew that if he hit me indoors, he would have been in trouble. Are the Italian laws so stupid that they let a grown man hit a child outdoors? My mother was screaming at him to leave me alone. At this point, I was laughing at him because he simply couldn't make any headway in getting me through the door. He must have come with the specific purpose of giving me a good hiding for not having obeyed his orders. Yes, he must have made himself look a fool in front of his son with me not obeying his commands.

Sometime later, my mother left with Antonio on his scooter and didn't return for a few days. I was surprised as normally, she would say that she would be going to see whoever for a few days. But to go with Antonio to his home for a few days must have meant that his wife wasn't there for this time. When she returned, she came by train and not with Antonio. That was another mystery. I preferred it that Antonio had not come.

*Many years later, my mother informed me that when Antonio drove off with her and wherein she was gone for several days, Antonio had, in fact, kidnapped her. Between him and his wife, they kept her in their flat tied up like a prisoner and insisted that she give them the money she received from the sale of the orchard. As luck would have it, his wife had to go out for some reason. She left with the scooter. While she was gone with the Vespa, she had an accident and broke a leg. Therefore, he was forced to go to the hospital, which was in the same town. That gave my mother the chance to free herself and get out of that place.*

*I never did ask my mother if I should have gotten some money for the three summers and two winters that I was in Siusi.*

Carla's family had moved from Egna to a village near Trento, and our meetings became constantly fewer. In Egna, I became fond of another girl. As I was just getting to know her, she ended up going to Brunico to work. These friendships were always a hidden affair because of my mother's attitude. Only Pino was allowed to have girlfriends, and a motorbike was bought for him while I had to hide my friendship with the girl I liked. Well, I had a friend in Egna, Gino, who had a moped, and we had good fun together. As my aunt lived in Egna, she saw me with my friend. Then later, when she saw my mother, she told her of my friendship with this boy who was one year older than me. All of a sudden, I was forbidden to frequent him. This was getting ridiculous. She was married and could choose her boyfriends as she desired. I was single and could not choose my own friends. I simply could not understand the mentality of my mother. At the age of seven, I was big enough to leave home to go and earn my daily bread. Then at fourteen, I was too young to choose my friends. To be placed in a position to keep a friendship hidden by my own mother must be wrong. From now on, I would have friends, and I would simply keep it hidden from my mother as much as possible.

Now my eyes opened to the fact that the war food shortage was long over. The three older brothers were, in fact, working on the construction sites and came home during the evening. Ignaz had by then obtained his apprenticeship position and was living in. Soon after I had come home from Siusi, I was sent to work with Giovanni, a local farmer. After that, I worked on the construction sites. Klaus was still in Siusi. It seemed to be perfectly arranged for my mother to do what she liked best during the day.

Somehow, Antonio's scooter ended up in our family for Lodovico. Lodovico had a girlfriend from a village about fifteen kilometers away. One day, he had an argument with my mother about Pino taking his girlfriend and getting a new motorbike while he received the old scooter. We boys had the duty to work and give up our money at home while my mother could control it to her heart's delight.

As the work was scarce in this area, Lodovoco was contemplating returning to Germany. I was really trying to find a mechanic's apprenticeship position. I went on my bike to the local mechanics and asked them if they had a vacant position for an apprentice. As they didn't have any vacancies, I went further afield to try the same thing. Every day, I had to cycle farther and farther. After a while of trying, I ended up in Merano. There, at long last, I could have had what I was looking for. When I was asked where I lived, I said I lived in Laghetti. The man in the workshop replied, "Laghetti is more the sixty kilometers from here. You wouldn't earn enough to pay for a room in this area, and to cycle more than 120 kilometers a day is simply not an option."

He had a valid point, which made me reflect. When I was nine years old and worked for nothing, they wouldn't even let me run away. Now, when I was thinking about my future, I couldn't find a position to learn what I would like to learn.

When I finished school, my teacher said something about me going to middle school. My mother wouldn't even discuss it. I was hesitant too. My reading was simply too bad for me to go to middle school. At that time, the middle school wasn't compulsory; therefore, I chose the easy way out. I was asking myself what I could study if I couldn't read.

In such a case, what chance would I have had of receiving some help with renting a room in Merano? Lodovico left for Germany. The scooter stayed behind, and I used it. At thirteen, I could drive a scooter with no driver's license. I did a few more jobs in the area of different sorts. On one job, I helped an insulator to insulate a cold storage area of a fruit storage and sorting complex. This person was using cork sheets, which were about eight centimeters thick and were 50 x 100 centimeters. These sheets were glued to the walls in several layers. Here, I got the same pay as a laborer. But here, there was a canteen, and for 100 Lire, I could receive a big plate of good tasting pasta. Then when this job came to an end, I had to start all over in finding something new.

I was slowly beginning to understand the attitude of my father. I could work and work, give the money to my mother, and she would never have any to spare if I wanted something. I think that my father, eventually in desperation, simply stopped giving money to my mother. This isn't an excuse for my father neglecting his fatherly duties.

I used the scooter regularly if I had to drive several kilometers. Thus, I was always broke. Still, during the school days, a bank employee came to the school to give a talk and leave each pupil with a metal savings box. Then, about once a year, I took it to the bank in Egna. There, they had the key to open the box, take out and count the money, and place it on the deposit account. Over the period, I ended up saving 7,000 Lire. That was the equivalent of seventy hours work as a laborer. That money would buy a pair of strong leather mountain boots, and I would have had 3,500 Lire left over. As saving this money was such an effort, it became something like a sacred article. It wasn't to be touched.

## Chapter Twenty-Two

MY MOTHER'S AUNT MARTA CAME to see us from Innsbruck. She didn't come to see only us; she also wanted to see my grandparents, who were her brother-in-law and his wife. While this aunt was with us, she had the idea that I should go to Innsbruck and get a job there. "You will not have any problem in finding a job there," was her belief. By now, Enzo's petrol station had opened. From here, many lorries would stop to fill up before going to the Brenner pass with the goods they had. Enzo assured me that he could ask some drivers that crossed the border to give me a lift to Innsbruck.

Well, if I really intended to go, I would have to apply for a passport. I went and informed myself about getting one. You know what? They wanted 6,000 Lire for a passport from a boy. That was a week's wages working ten hours a day— and before expenses. It seemed like a fortune to me to pay so much for a passport to a nation that couldn't even teach me to read. My mother made a fuss about giving me the money for this exorbitant expense. I had the photos made at an additional expense, and I applied for the passport. I did have to wait for a few weeks to receive it.

Exactly one month before my fifteenth birthday, on September 15, 1957, early evening, my mother and I went to Enzo's petrol station. Then, when a specific lorry came that drove to the Innsbruck fruit market, I got a lift on it. Now, as there was enough room in the cabin, my mother decided to come too. On the way, I had a feeling just like the one I had when I first went "Ai Freschi," a feeling of going into the unknown. We crossed the Brenner border after midnight and got to the Innsbruck market during the night. My mother left after a few days. I found a job with a local building company and lived with Marta, aunt of my mother.

My dreams for the future would now start from there.

.........................................................................

*I would like to thank Barbara Mahlknecht (http://www.grunserhof.com/) and Claudio Paterno for supplying the photos of the Siusi Alps in the Bolzano Dolomites region of Italy, which is, without doubt, one of the most beautiful regions on our globe.*

www.ingramcontent.com/pod-product-compliance
Lightning Source LLC
Chambersburg PA
CBHW061525050726
47593CB00002B/669

* 9 7 8 1 9 5 1 3 0 2 3 6 8 *